THE WRITING PROGRAMME ● ●

WRITE ALONG

PATRICK LASHMAR / DAVID W. BOOTH ✴✴✴✴ Nancy O'Neill / Meguido Zola

Globe/Modern Curriculum Press
Toronto

Canadian Cataloguing in Publication Data

Lashmar, Patrick.
    Write along

(The Writing programme)
For use in elementary schools.
Includes index.
ISBN 0-88996-088-7

1. English language — Composition and exercises.
I. Booth, David W. (David Wallace), 1938-
II. Title. III. Series.

PE1408.L27 1983   808'.042   C83-098990-0

Editor: Elma Schemenauer
Designer: John Zehethofer

Thanks to the following reviewers for their valuable
comments and suggestions:

Margaret O. Crocker, Halifax
Jean Hoeft, Calgary
Elizabeth R. King, Waterloo
Peter King, Ottawa

Photographs:
Page 109 — Robert S. Schemenauer
Illustrations:
Pages 26, 27 — Hope Mount

Printed and bound in Canada
by John Deyell Company

0 9 8 7 6 5 4 3 2

ABOUT THIS BOOK

- "Write me a letter."
- "Let's write a scary story."
- "When I express my feelings in a poem, I understand myself better."
- "She wrote out directions telling us how to get to the library."

Writing is important in our lives today. This book will give you many ideas for writing in different ways. It will encourage you to express yourself and communicate with others.

Do you ever have trouble writing? In *The Writing Programme* you will find many interesting selections to give you ideas for your own writing. There are stories, poems, interviews, recipes, cartoons, announcements, scripts, and many more — all chosen especially for you.

The Writing Programme gives you easy-to-understand suggestions about how to plan, revise, edit, and share your writing. You will read some of your writing aloud. You will listen to other students read to the class or to groups or on tape. You will discuss . . . speak . . . role-play . . . dramatize . . . look at interesting pictures and diagrams . . . and prepare your own illustrations and displays as well.

Throughout the book you will be reminded of things to look for in composing and improving your writing. Choice of words, imagination, colourful comparisons, accuracy, good paragraphing, punctuation, spelling, and handwriting all play a part in making writing effective. The checklists on page 136 will help you edit your own work and the work of others. The author/title index lists the selections found in the book, and the names of their authors. The subject index tells you where you can find the different topics that are discussed.

The most important part of this book is your own writing. You will have a chance to write about your own experiences and feelings, about things that you imagine, and about things that you have observed and learned. Writing helps you understand yourself and the world around you. And it is an important way of sharing and communicating.

CONTENTS

SHARING EXPERIENCES

TRUE STORIES

Do you like to read true stories about the lives of famous people in magazines like television guides? Why do we want to know so many details about a famous person's life? You can write a true story about a relative, a friend, or an interesting person in your neighbourhood. You can interview the person, interview people who know the person, and then write the biography. You can illustrate your biography with photos or drawings. What information does the picture give you about the following true story?

from **A prairie boy's summer**
by William Kurelek

Milking Time

Milking was a job William didn't look forward to, especially on hot, fly-filled days.

Outside there might be a blue sky and perhaps a refreshing breeze, but inside, the barn was like a furnace. To get at the teats on the far side of the cow's udder he had to lean tight against the cow's belly, which heaved and radiated heat like a big oven. Adding to the discomfort of the sweat, flies used his head and hands as a landing field. William had to be ready to grab the pail of milk away in case the cow kicked at a fly and put her foot in the pail. She used her tail as a fly swatter, too; and its coarse, dirty hairs often slapped William right across the back of the neck. He'd spray the cow with flytox, but its effect soon wore off. It was best when his little sister Nancy held the tail.

As relief from the milking ordeal, William amused himself by squirting one of the barn cats that waited near by, meow-

ing for its evening ration. It would jump away as if upset, but really it liked the white shower; for it sat down further off and set about licking away the milk.

If William's mother — who was the best milker in the family — was away for some reason it meant he and John had ten cows each to milk. That night their wrists would ache so badly they couldn't sleep. Everybody was relieved when the family became prosperous enough to buy a set of milking machines.

1. What did you learn from reading this biography? Is this interesting information to put in a biography? Why?
2. This biography was really written by the author about himself. William Kurelek was a famous Canadian painter. Why do you think he called himself "he" instead of "I?"
3. If your wishes could come true, who are the people you would like to meet so that you could write biographies of them?
4. Should you get a person's permission before writing a biography? What if they have already died?

THE WRITING WORKSHOP

Get Ready

"Milking Time" is a true story. It is about William and a job he didn't like — milking the cows. What didn't he like about his job? Brainstorm jobs that you do not like. Why do you dislike them?

Start Writing

Everyone in a family has certain jobs to do. We do not always enjoy all the work we do to help our family. But we do it anyway. It is important for everyone in a family to do his or her fair share of the work. Is there a member of your family who dislikes one of his or her jobs? Maybe your:

- older brother hates to take the garbage out
- little brother dislikes setting the table
- sister dislikes cleaning out the tropical fish tank

Write a true story about someone in your family. Tell about a job they don't look forward to. You will be writing the story for this person to read. Make the story funny if you can.

Edit Your Work

A. Look over your first copy, or **draft**. Did you say clearly what you wanted to say? Did you write the events in order?

B. With a partner take turns editing your stories. Use these steps:

1) Read the story silently to enjoy it and to get the main ideas.

2) Read the story aloud to your partner. Then correct any errors you noticed when reading aloud.

C. 1) Sentences are made up of words. Each word in a sentence has a job to do. It has a function. As we edit our writing, it is helpful to be able to talk about the words we use in our sentences. We need to be able to decide whether or not certain words are doing a good job in a sentence. To help us talk about the different kinds of words in sentences, we have names for them, depending on the job each does. One kind of word has the job of naming. **Naming words** give names to people, places, and things. *Albert, Ottawa,* and *snowmobile* are all naming words, or **nouns**. Selecting naming words carefully can make our writing more accurate and/or more interesting.

2) List five naming words, or nouns, used in "Milking Time." Are any of these especially unusual or interesting? Why?

3) Underline the naming words that you used in your story. Are they the best ones you can think of? For example, are they accurate? Are some of them especially interesting for one reason or another?

D. Now write the final draft of your story.

Use The Language Arts

A. Give your story to the family member you wrote about, and let him or her read it. Talk with the person about your story.

B. Now that you have written a true story about someone in your family, give him or her a chance to write about you. Ask the person to write a true story about you. You may be very interested to read what he or she writes!

A **writing folder** is an excellent place to keep your writing. You will want to keep some of your best pieces of writing in it so that you or other people can enjoy reading them later. You can also use it for the writing you are working on, but have not finished. Begin your folder. You may want to put your story in it.

SHARING EXPERIENCES

LOGS

A captain of a ship must, by law, keep a log of each day's happenings at sea. A log is like a calendar of events. You can keep a day-by-day account of what happens in your life. You can record and enter in your log what you experience and observe. You can use drawings as well to note your discoveries. The log that follows is about the life of a field mouse.

from Wild mouse
by Irene Brady

April 6.   *I've just seen a wild mouse —
smooth, sleek, darting across the sink top.
I'm going to try to sketch him.*

April 14.   *I'm trying to win the mouse's
confidence with cornflakes and apple
chunks. If I'm very quiet he stays in sight
long enough for me to sketch a little.*

April 20. *Two weeks of constant coaxing, but it was worth it. He sat and ate sunflower seeds in my hand tonight, but when I moved slightly he was gone! What a delightful feeling, those tickly toes on my palm!*

April 30. *He's getting so tubby I can't believe it! Maybe I should stop feeding him, but he's so beautiful to watch (even though he is fat). . . . He's building a nest someplace. He's made a total wreck of the toilet paper roll.*

May 5. *He is a she! I pulled out the drawer of the coffee mill because I heard scratching inside and I'm watching a small miracle. She chewed a hole in the back of the mill, built a snug nest, and is crouched in its hollow having babies. One tiny red thing lies beside her and another seems to be coming. The mother is ignoring me. She's busy.*

1. What do you think will be recorded next in the log about the field mouse?
2. How is a log different from a diary?
3. Discuss: "What would happen if animals kept logs of their observations of humans?"
4. What kinds of logs would you like to discover in an old book shop?
5. How do logs from long ago help us understand what life was like then? Find examples of logs in the library. Notice their language and the events they describe.

THE WRITING WORKSHOP

Get Ready

Irene Brady's log records things that actually happened. She wrote her true story in many parts. Each part was written on a different day. Read her log again and talk about it.

Start Writing

Begin your own log today. Write it so that your family will be interested in reading it. Use this plan to write your log:

1) Write in your log each day for seven days.

2) Write your log about anything you find interesting. Irene Brady kept a log about a wild mouse. You can use one of these topics if you like:

- My Pet — Describe the activities of the family pet.
- Lunching and Munching — Record and describe everything you eat each day.
- Dressing for All Occasions — Keep a log of the clothes you wear each day.
- My Brother or Sister — Record and describe interesting things this person does each day.

3) Write each day. You may write as little as a few sentences, or a whole page if you like.

4) What you write should tell a true story.

5) Write the date at the top of each log entry.

Edit Your Work

A. **Revise** your log, using these steps. The first time, read it to enjoy the true story you have written. Now read your log a second time and think about these questions:

1) Is everything I wrote about my topic?

2) Is everything I wrote true?

3) Did I remember to put the date at the top of each log entry?

4) Do all of my sentences make sense?

5) Is there anything I should change so that my family will understand what I have written?

B. Edit your log with a partner by using these questions:

1) Do all of the sentences make sense?

2) Is each sentence punctuated correctly?

3) Are all the words spelled correctly?

C. We use **capital letters**:

1) to begin the first word of a sentence

2) for names of people and pets

3) for names of places such as streets, cities, and countries

4) for names of days of the week, months, and holidays

5) for titles

6) for the word *I*

Read your log once more to see that you have used capital letters correctly. Make any needed changes.

Use The Language Arts

A. Take your log home. Gather your family together and read it to them.

B. The last entry in Irene Brady's log was written on May 5. She probably wrote other entries after May 5. Pretend you are Irene. What do you think happened to the mother mouse and her babies? Write a log entry for each of these dates: May 12, May 17, May 24, and June 1.

C. Begin to keep a journal. You can write in it every day. Your journal will become a special book about you. If you write in your journal every day, you will soon have written a whole book.

(A journal is much like a log. But it is usually more personal, and contains information on a wider variety of subjects.)

9

SHARING EXPERIENCES

FRIENDLY LETTERS

It is fun to keep in touch with people who are far away by sending letters. When you write to a friend, it is like having a conservation. You can tell your friend what has happened in your life, and you can ask about his or her life. Also, you can reread old letters when you feel lonely, and remember your friend. What does this letter tell you about Maryanne's life?

from Pioneer girl
by Maryanne Caswell

January 1, 1888

Dear Grandma,

Next day was dull and mild. Father had gone for hay. We were returning from the river waterhole with the cattle when we saw flames leaping from the stove-pipe in the roof of our sod house. We ran with all speed. Mother was just finishing the wash and could not believe us as the fire was low. But as the sight soon convinced her she threw salt into the stove, sent Martha to the roof while Jen and John carried water to me at the ladder, Martha getting it to the top. We finally with salt, water, beating and stuffing with a mat, got it under control. Mother's strength then seemed to desert her. When father came there was a discussion of ways and means to build a chimney for safety and to stop the continual dripping of soot.

We got in a barrel, filled it with frozen clay dug from the well; as this thawed we spaded it fine and mixed with chaff. Father made a brace for the chimney so we have a book shelf, and a place for the water pail below. We carried the

10

mixed clay while father each night added a bit till finished.

Last night at midnight, father went out and fired off the musket into the air. Uncle Joe, on his way to celebrate, shot a rabbit which he left for us. Mother and I like rabbit, but the others, ugh! For dinner mother cooked the last of our salted cod fish, potatoes in their skin, dried raspberries, cooked or stewed johnny cake.

Before dark we found a new calf in the stable so now we will have plenty of milk in the new year though another cow dropped dead on the way to the river yesterday.

It is shovelling snow, bucking, cutting or sawing wood, mending ox-harness, setting and sharpening the bucksaw, driving cattle to the river watering-hole, cutting and cleaning it out, hauling water out of the well, feeding the stock, cleaning the stable and chicken house, riding the pony on the threshing floor, helping unload hay, teaching the pups to heel and "lie down dead," reading out loud in the firelight, seeing pictures in the flames, off to bed and sleep to be up early to begin the new year of 1888. What will it have for us?

Happy New Year to all.

Your granddaughter,

Maryanne

---

1. What kinds of things is the writer talking to her grandmother about in her letter? Could the same letter be written today?
2. If you were writing a letter to a friend about last New Year's Eve, what would you say? What special things about the way you celebrate New Year's could you describe to your friend?
3. Do you ever have trouble knowing what to say in a letter?

THE WRITING WORKSHOP

Get Ready

Today we often talk to our friends and relatives on the telephone. Before the telephone was invented, people would communicate with faraway friends and loved ones mostly by letter. In Maryanne's letter, written in 1888, she talks to her grandmother.

1) What are two things Maryanne talks to her grandmother about in this letter?

2) A friendly letter has five parts: date, greeting, body, closing, and signature. Find these in Maryanne's letter.

Start Writing

Today many people still write letters to friends and relatives when they want to talk to them. Write a letter to one of your grandparents, or another person in your family that you love very much. Try to write to someone who lives in another community. Do a good job because you are going to mail the letter when it is finished.

Edit Your Work

A. Improve the first **draft** of your letter, using these steps:

1) Read your letter twice to yourself. The first time, read it to see if you are happy with what you said. Should you add anything?

2) Now read your letter a second time, thinking about these questions.
- Did you use commas after the date, greeting, and closing?
- Do all of your sentences make sense?
- Is there anything you should change so that your relative will more easily understand your letter?
- Does the letter follow the correct form?

B. 1) A **period** is a punctuation mark that is used:
- at the end of a statement sentence
- after abbreviations
- after initials

2) Read your letter once again to make sure you used periods correctly.

C. The letter you wrote is special because you wrote it for a special person. To make sure your relative can read this letter easily, copy it out in your best handwriting.

Now put your letter in an envelope. Address it, using the form below.

Patrick D. Kennedy
119 James St.
Grand Falls, Nfld.
L8N 3T4

　　　　　　　Mr. Brian Kennedy
　　　　　　　12 Smallwood Rd.
　　　　　　　St. John's, Nfld.
　　　　　　　L8N 4S2

Put your envelope in the mailbox and get ready for an answer.

Use The Language Arts

A. Write a thank you note. In this kind of letter, you thank someone for something they have given you or done for you. Think of someone you should thank, and send them a thank you note.

You might:
- thank a relative for a present you received
- thank a friend for getting you out of a jam
- thank your coach for helping you improve in a sport such as hockey

B. Have you read any stories or novels in which the author uses letters as part of the book? Make a bulletin board display of "Letters from Literature."

AUTOBIOGRAPHIES

The person that you can write about most easily is probably yourself. When you write about your own life, you are writing an autobiography. You can organize your writing by telling about things that have happened in the past, things that are happening in the present, and things you hope will happen in the future. In the following selection, the author describes an evening in her home as a Japanese-Canadian child.

from A child in prison camp
by Shizuye Takashima

Our home at night

It is night. We light our two candles.
There is no electricity.
The frail, rationed candles burst into life and the darkness slinks away. The smell of fresh cut trees burning fills the room. The pine pitch cracks and pops in the fire. I sit, watch my mother.
She places the rice pot on the black, heavy stove.
The wet, shiny pot begins to sputter.
''Rice tastes better cooked like this,'' she says, and smiles. Her dark eyes look even darker in this semi-light and I feel love for her. ''Why?'' I ask. ''Because natural fire is best for cooking. Food tastes pure.''
I stare at the now boiling rice and wonder why all people do not use such stoves and fuel.

Yuki brings wood. I help her pile it near the
hot stove, for the raw wood is damp.
The family who share the kitchen, the stove, and

the house begin their dinner. I pile the wood.
The white part of the wood looks strange in
this dim light. Some of the pitch sticks to our hands. I
look at the sticky, yellow liquid coming out of the wood.
Kay-ko stares at it.
"What is it? It smells funny." I reply,
"It's pitch. Comes from the pine tree.
We learned this in school."
Yuki joins in and adds, "It's the sap of the tree.
It's full of the sun's energy. This is why it
cracks and pops as it burns." Kay-ko and I both
listen, and we hear the sharp snap of the pitch
burning. The fresh smell of the pine reaches us.
We both wrinkle our noses. Kay-ko laughs.
I dab a bit of soft pitch on her nose; she does
the same to me. Soon we forget all about piling
the wood and end up laughing and laughing.

The table is set; the white candles create a circle
of light on the wood table. I sit by the flame.
I notice the far corners of the room are dark. This
gives an eerie feeling. But my eyes and mind are getting
used to this kind of light.

---

1. What have you learned about the author of this autobiography?
2. Is the author talking about modern life, or life in the past? How can you tell?
3. How did this family make do without electricity? How would your life be different if you had no electricity?
4. What autobiographies have you read?
5. Brainstorm other ways you can tell about your life, other than in an autobiography.

THE WRITING WORKSHOP

Get Ready

There are many ways you can write an autobiography. Some autobiographies are short. They tell only a few important details about a person's life. Others are long, and tell many details. Look back at the selection from Shizuye Takashima's autobiography. What does she tell about her home? members of her family?

Start Writing

Write your autobiography for your family to read. It will be a true story about you and your family. Your family will be interested in reading it because they are interested in you. Even though they will already know some of the facts, they will be interested in your point of view. There are many ways you can write an autobiography. This time, write your autobiography using this plan:

1) *In your first paragraph* write about your past:
  • when and where you were born
  • interesting things that happened to you as you were growing up

2) *In your second paragraph* tell about your family:
  • how many are in your family
  • the names and ages of your brothers and sisters
  • something interesting about someone in your family

3) *In your third paragraph* tell about your school:
  • name, address, and telephone number of your school
  • teacher's name and principal's name
  • what you like best about learning

4) *In your fourth paragraph* tell about interesting things in your life:
  • your friends
  • your hobbies
  • your favourite games and TV shows
  • other things you like

Edit Your Work

A. Improve your first **draft** using these questions:
1) Did I say clearly what I wanted to say?
2) Did I include the most important information?
3) Did I use the most interesting words I could think of?

B. Exchange your autobiography with a friend. Your friend will enjoy reading your true story. He or she can help you edit it so that your family will be sure to understand what you wrote.
   A good way to help each other is to:
1) Read the autobiography once to enjoy it.
2) Read it a second time and edit it, using these questions:
 • Does the autobiography follow the plan?
 • Are time clues and words used correctly to tell about the past, the present, and the future?
 • Does every sentence make sense?

C. A **sentence** is a group of words that tells who or what does something. Read your autobiography once more to make sure you used complete sentences.

Use The Language Arts

A. Autobiographies are enjoyable because people's lives are interesting to read about.

1) Share your story with four other students. Place all five autobiographies on a desk face down. Pick one from the pile. Each person in the group will read aloud the story he or she picked.

2) Take your autobiography home and read it to your entire family. Then show it to them and talk about it.

B. Have an autobiography festival for two weeks in your class. Class members take turns reading autobiographical stories about famous people. You may find your stories in books, magazines, or newspapers.

RULES

Many young people think they have to follow too many rules in life. However, rules are a means of keeping order in our world, so that society can run smoothly. Some rules are written down; others are unwritten, but we know that we must obey them.

House rules for an Alberta hotel in 1880

1. Charges as follows:
   Board, $25 a month.
   Board and lodging with wooden bench to sleep on, $50 a month.
   Board and lodging with a bed, $60 a month.
   No Jawbone. In God we trust; all others cash.
2. The adjacent vacant lot is available as sleeping accommodation to guests without baggage.
3. Before retiring at night spiked boots and spurs must be removed.
4. Dogs may sleep beneath the bunks but are not allowed *in* the bunks. Only one dog per single room.
5. The hour of rising is 6:00 a.m. This is very important as the sheets are required for tablecloths.
6. For the use of hot water, soap, candles, or other luxuries, there will be an extra charge. When guests leave they will receive a rebate on all or parts of candles not burned or eaten.
7. Baths may be had free at the river. Soap and insect powder may be purchased from the bar; towels will be changed once a week.
8. Valuables such as jewelry will not be locked away in the safe. This establishment has no such gem.

9. Guests are strictly prohibited from striking matches or spitting on the ceiling.
10. Breakfast and dinner will be provided, but guests must rustle up their own lunch.
11. No complaining with regard to the food. Guests will be put out if they do not like what is provided or how much.
12. Assaults on the cook are strictly forbidden.
13. When guests request meals to be served in bedrooms, the management provides no guarantee. Our waiters are not above temptation and seem to be a hungry lot.
14. Do not tip directly to the waiters or servants. Give the tip to the proprietor, who will then distribute the money — if he considers it necessary.
15. Shots through the door panel will bring the waiter. Two shots for ice water, three if you need a new deck of cards.
16. The management will not be held responsible for anything. In the event of a fire, guests are to leave without further ado.
17. We do not cash cheques for anyone. We accept payment only if it is made in Cash, Gold Dust, or Blue Chips.
18. If a guest finds himself or his baggage thrown over the fence, he may consider he has received notice to leave.

---

1. Do hotels have rules today? Do they publish their rules for people to see?
2. Do you think these were the actual rules in 1880? What is the author poking fun at?
3. How do you think rules should be decided upon? Who should make them? When should rules be changed?
4. What groups in society help us to obey the rules? Does society appreciate these people?
5. In groups, create a scene in which a hotel keeper asks some guests to leave because they have broken the rules.

THE WRITING WORKSHOP

Get Ready

What rules for an Alberta hotel did you find most interesting? Why? Do you think this list of rules is real or made up? Which rules seem real? Which ones seem to have been made up? Have you ever stayed in a hotel or a motel? Are there house rules for modern hotels and motels?

Start Writing

Every school has rules. These rules are not always listed on a special notice and hung up in the halls. But they exist just the same. For example, maybe class members take turns watering the plants in the classroom. What are the rules in your school? Write them down. You are writing them for other students to read and think about. Use this plan:

1) Think of rules about how you act:
- on the playground
- in the hall
- in class
- with teachers and other students

2) Write in complete sentences.
3) Number each rule.

Edit Your Work

A. Look at your first **draft** again. Are there any important rules that you left out? Are all of your rules written so that they are easy to understand?

B. In groups of four, share your list of school rules. Take turns reading your lists. They will not be the same. What rules should you add to your list? Did you list statements that the others in your group do not think of as rules? Talk about these.

In your groups, edit your work. Each person in the group

can read all four lists of rules for a specific reason. Decide which group member will perform each of these editing jobs:
- Edit your spelling.
- Edit to see that each sentence makes sense.
- Edit to see that capital letters and periods have been used correctly.
- Edit to see that no unnecessary words have been used.

C. These rules should be written in **sentences**. A group of words that tells a complete thought is called a **sentence**. Make sure you wrote all your rules in sentence form. Now write your second draft, making any necessary changes.

Use The Language Arts

A. There are eighteen house rules listed for the Alberta Hotel. Make up six more rules that you think are funny. Add these to the list.

B. Write a modern version of "House Rules for an Alberta Hotel."

C. Hold a class discussion on why it is important to have rules at school.

1) In groups of four, take turns reading your lists of school rules.

2) Decide as a group on what you think are the three most important school rules. When you decide, choose a recorder to write these down.

3) Discuss why each rule is necessary. The recorder will list two or three reasons for each.

4) Select a reporter to present your group's ideas to the class.

5) Each reporter will read his or her group's report. All members of the group will help to answer any questions the other students may have.

(Are you remembering to write in the journal that you began in the Sharing Experiences section?)

INSTRUCTIONS

Do you have a hobby? How did you learn the information about your hobby? People who become experts in their field often write books of instructions for those who are beginning. The following instructions are about people collecting rocks — just to enjoy them.

from Everybody needs a rock
by Byrd Baylor

Everybody
needs
a rock.

I'm sorry for kids
who don't have
a rock
for a friend.

I'm sorry for kids
who only have
TRICYCLES
BICYCLES
HORSES
ELEPHANTS
GOLDFISH
THREE-ROOM PLAYHOUSES
FIRE ENGINES
WIND-UP DRAGONS
AND THINGS LIKE THAT
if
they don't have
a

rock
for a friend.

That's why
I'm giving them
my own
RULES
for
finding
a
rock . . .

Not
just
any rock.
I mean
a
special
rock
that you find
yourself
and keep
as long as

you can —
maybe
forever.

If somebody says,
"What's so speical
about that rock?"
don't even tell them.
I don't.

Nobody
is supposed
to know
what's special
about
another person's
rock.

All right.
Here
are
the
rules:

RULE NUMBER 1

If you can,
go to a mountain
made out of
nothing but
a hundred million
small
shiny
beautiful
roundish
rocks.

But if you can't,
any place will do.
Even an alley.
Even a sandy road.
. . . .

RULE NUMBER 2

The shape
of the rock
is up to you.
(There is a girl in Alaska
who only likes flat rocks.
Don't ask me why.
I like them lumpy.)

The thing to remember
about shapes
is this:
Any rock
looks good
with a hundred other rocks
around it on a hill.
But
if your rock
is going to be special
it should look good
by itself
in the bathtub.

---

1. Why do you think the author began to care about rocks?
2. Why does the author want us to collect and enjoy rocks?
3. What do you think the author's other rules about rocks will be concerned with?
4. What style has the author chosen for giving directions?
5. Is "love of nature" disappearing from our world?
6. In groups, prepare one rule as a choral speaking selection. Who would be saying this? Why? To whom?

THE WRITING WORKSHOP

Get Ready

A. When are written directions easy to follow? What can make written directions difficult to follow?

Why is it important that directions be:
- in order?
- complete?
- clear?
- exact?
- accurate?

B. **Time-order words** are used in directions to organize the steps in the proper sequence. Read these time-order words:
- first
- as
- next
- after
- while
- second
- now
- then

Brainstorm a list of at least five more time-order words.

Start Writing

Now it is your turn to write directions for another person. Think about something you know how to do very well, but that the other person does not know how to do. There are many things you can do well. Select one. Or use the list below to help you.
- looking after plants
- caring for your pet
- making your bed
- finding a book in the library
- making breakfast

Decide whom you are writing the directions for. You can give the directions to that person when you are finished.

Use the writing plan below.

1) State the purpose of your directions.

2) Write everything in the correct order.

3) Use time-order words.

4) Do not leave out any important steps.

5) Avoid unnecessary words.

6) Write in complete sentences.

7) Make sure each sentence is easy to understand.

Edit Your Work

A. Look again at your first **draft**. Use the writing plan above to improve your work.

B. Each word in a sentence has a job to do. As we edit our writing, it is helpful to be able to talk about the words we use. We must be able to talk about whether or not certain words are doing a good job in a sentence. We have names for words, depending on the job each does.

We learned earlier about naming words, or nouns. We learned that the job of nouns in sentences is to name people, places, and things. **Action words** do a different job. They show action in a sentence. *Mix, fall,* and *race* can be action words. Selecting action words, or **verbs**, carefully can make our writing more accurate and more interesting.

With a partner, read your directions again. Do all the action words in your directions give a clear picture of the action? Should some be replaced with more effective ones? With your partner, edit your directions to make sure you have used the best possible action words, or verbs.

Use The Language Arts

A. Give your directions to the person for whom you wrote them. Ask the person to do the activity. If you wrote good directions and if the person can follow directions well, then he or she should be able to do it.

B. You may wish to create a poster advertising the hobby of rock collecting, or some other hobby that you like.

GAMES

The same games are often played in many different countries of the world. How does this happen? How does a game travel around the world? There can be many forms of one game. Here are three versions of *statues*.

Statues 1

The person who is "it" acts as a puller. He or she takes a player's hand and whirls him or her around. When "it" lets go, the player must "freeze" in the position in which he or she stops. The puller whirls each player around. All players "freeze." Then, the first one to move becomes "it."

Statues 2

Once the statues are "frozen," the puller can walk around and talk to them. He or she can make funny faces to try to make them laugh.

Statues 3

Once the players are in position, the person who is "it" can tell each of them to "be" something. For example, "it" might tell one person to be a beaver; another, a chicken; another, a robot; and so on. Then the puller says "Statues move." The statues come to life and begin moving like whatever they were told to "be." When "it" says "Statues freeze," the players stop in their positions. The puller decides whose position is best. That person becomes the new "it."

1. Why do games play such an important part in our lives?
2. What other games involve "freezing" and not moving as part of the instructions?
3. Notice the style in which these games are written. Can you rewrite them another way?
4. What statues can be seen in your community?
5. Create a group statue of a famous event. Write the instructions for creating the scene. Try not titling your instructions, and having another group follow them. Can the group guess what event they are showing?

THE WRITING WORKSHOP

Get Ready

If possible, play a game of *statues* as a class. With your teacher, brainstorm a list of games on the chalkboard. Organize the games by type. Use these headings. (Some examples are given.)

SPORTS	CARD GAMES	VIDEO GAMES	WORD GAMES	BOARD GAMES	RUNNING GAMES
Volleyball	Fish	Star Strike	Password	Monopoly	Frozen Tag
Hockey	31	Smurf Action Game	Scrabble	Chess	Dragon Tag

Talk about the games you play by thinking about these questions:

- What games do you enjoy the most?
- Whom do you play these games with?

Start Writing

Write the directions for playing one of your favourite games. Select a game that you know well and that is not too complicated to describe. You are writing the directions so you can play the game with someone.

Use this writing plan:

1) Make rough notes in point form, describing step by step how to play the game.

2) Review your rough notes to see that you haven't left out any important steps.

3) Now rewrite your directions. Make them easy to understand.

4) Write your directions in order, using time-order words.

5) Write in complete sentences.

Edit Your Work

A. Read your first **draft** again to see if you can make it better. When we do this, we are **revising** our work.

B. Knowing the **four kinds of sentences** and being able to use them helps you make your writing more interesting. It helps you add variety to your writing.

1) A **statement sentence** tells something. It ends in a period. Example: *The girls played hockey.*

2) A **question sentence** asks a question. It ends with a question mark. Example: *Does your family enjoy playing Monopoly?*

3) A **command sentence** gives a command. It ends with a period or an exclamation mark. Examples: *Start the game. Quit cheating at chess!*

4) An **exclamation sentence** shows strong feelings such as anger, excitement, or surprise. It ends with an exclamation mark. Example: *We won the game!*

With a partner edit your game directions once more. Probably many of your sentences are commands. See if you can make your directions more interesting by using some question, statement, or exclamation sentences as well.

Use The Language Arts

A. Share your game directions with someone in your family. If they do not know the game, let them figure out how to play it by reading your directions. Play the game with them.

B. With a partner or a small group, make up a game. You can use ideas from games you already know. Write down the directions for your game. Make any pieces that are necessary. When you are finished, explain to the class how to play your game.

When you write in your journal, you might sometimes write about games that you like to play, new games you have learned, and the people you like to play games with.

This alphabet book is also a *rebus*. A rebus is a puzzle in which pictures, letters, or drawings are arranged to suggest words or syllables. Perhaps a letter of the alphabet may say its name as part of the puzzle.

U R YY 4 ME reads: You are too wise for me.

from From A to Z:
The collected letters of Irene and Hallie Coletta

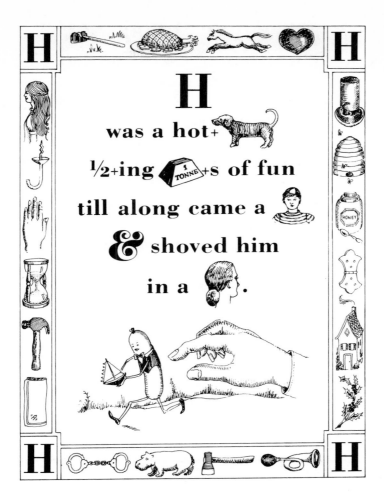

H
was a hot+ [dog]
½+ing [1 TONNE]+s of fun
till along came a [boy]
& shoved him
in a [bun].

---

1. Can you figure out all the rebus puzzles?
2. Can you explain the pictures in the margins around each letter?
3. Do you know any other codes or word puzzles?
4. How do word puzzles help us become better users of language?

THE WRITING WORKSHOP

Get Ready

How is an alphabet story different from most stories you read? What is its pattern? Do you enjoy reading stories that use pictures in place of words? Why? Do you remember what a rebus is?

Start Writing

Write an alphabet story using pictures in place of some words. Everyone in the class will write one or two parts of this story. Use this plan:

1) Decide on one or two letters of the alphabet to write about. Try not to use the same letters as other students in your class.

2) Choose topics that start with your letters. Example: A — apple, B — buffalo

3) Make up an interesting sentence to tell about your topic. Use words and pictures in this sentence.

Edit Your Work

A. Describing words help to make writing more exact and more interesting. Some **describing words** tell about a person, place, or thing. What are the describing words in the examples?

- clever child
- small village
- red bicycle

A describing word that tells about a person, place, or thing may also be called an **adjective**.

Some describing words tell about actions. What are the describing words in these examples?

- eat slowly
- watch closely

A describing word that tells about an action may also be called an **adverb**.

If we know how to recognize and use describing words, then we can talk about them. We can talk about whether or not the describing words are doing a good job in the sentence.

Read your alphabet story once more. Can you make your story more interesting or accurate through your use of describing words?

B. Write your alphabet story again, making any changes you think will improve it. Use a full sheet of paper to do this. Print the words in large letters and draw your pictures carefully.

Use The Language Arts

A rebus is a puzzle in which pictures, letters, or drawings stand for words or syllables. Morse code is a way of sending messages in which dots and dashes stand for letters.

Here is the Morse code alphabet.

A . —	N — .	1 . — — — —
B — . . .	O — — —	2 . . — — —
C — . — .	P . — — .	3 . . . — —
D — . .	Q — — . —	4 . . . . —
E .	R . — .	5 . . . . .
F . . — .	S . . .	6 — . . . .
G — — .	T —	7 — — . . .
H	U . . —	8 — — — . .
I . .	V . . . —	9 — — — — .
J . — — —	W . — —	0 — — — — —
K — . —	X — . . —	
L . — . .	Y — . — —	
M — —	Z — — . .	

1) Use Morse code to write your name.

2) What does this message say?

— . .   — — —   — — .   . . .

. — . .   . .   — . —   .

— . . .   — — —   — .   . . . .

RIDDLES

"What lives in winter, dies in summer, and grows with its roots upwards?"

The answer to the riddle is "an icicle." Riddles are fun to create, and fun to try and answer. Each riddle has a telling part that gives clues, and an asking part. Can you solve the following riddles?

from Once there were dragons
by John Mole and Mary Norman

The nastier the day
The nicer we are to know;
We're a kind, you might say,
Of aerial raincoat
Or a rooftop on the go
Or even, stretching it,
The back of a duck.

Some of us will almost fit
Your pocket. Others
Can bring bad luck.

Whatever the time and place,
We're an open or shut case.

What is this?
by Miriam Young

A dragon travels underground.
I know because I've heard the sound
Of angry roaring that he makes,
And noticed how the platform shakes.
His breath is hot; I've seen the spark
As he comes rushing through the dark.
He stops — and there's a dreadful pause
As sideways *open all his jaws.*
He swallows people up and then
His jaws come sliding closed again.
He gives a smoky, dusty cough
And, red tail flashing, rumbles off.

A subway

Some traditional riddles from Newfoundland

Riddle me, riddle me, what is that,
Over the head and under the hat?   — The hair

What goes up the hill and down the hill,
And spite of all, yet standeth still?   — The road

What goes over the water and under the water
And never touches the water?   — An egg inside a duck

What stands on one leg with its heart in its head?
                                                      — Cabbage

What is that which belongs to you
But others use it more than you do?   — Your name

What has a tongue and cannot talk?   — Shoe

What has an eye and cannot see?   — Needle

I went into the woods and got it;
I sat down to look for it;
The more I looked for it, the less I liked it;
Not being able to find it, I came home with it.
                                                — Thorn in foot

---

1. What clues help you solve the riddles in the two poems?
2. The riddle poems are really comparison poems. How do comparisons help us understand things more clearly?
3. Why are so many fairy tales and folktales about the solving of riddles?
4. How is a mystery story like a riddle?

THE WRITING WORKSHOP

Get Ready

Did you enjoy reading the riddle poems on page 34? Why? These poems used interesting **comparisons** to help describe their subjects. Talk about the comparisons used in these poems. Which one did you find more interesting? Why?

Start Writing

Try to describe your hand using as many interesting comparisons as you can think of. You are writing this description for your teacher.

To begin, look at your hand and try to see it differently than you have ever seen it before. A hand is a hand, you say? Let's really look at it! Brainstorm interesting details about hands; for example, the fact that hair does not grow on the palms of people's hands. Talk about the different parts of the hand.

Think about what each of these parts is like. To what could you compare each part? Your teacher may want to list suggested comparisons on the chalkboard beside the names of the parts.

Examples:

Finger

- My fingers look like bare old tree trunks.
- My fingers are like chubby earthworms that have had a bath.
- My fingers can march like soldier going off to war.
- My fingers can dance like leaves in an April breeze.

Using the comparisons on the chalkboard and others you can think of, write a paragraph to describe your hand.

Begin your paragraph with the following sentences if you wish.

A hand is a hand, you say? This is not true of my hand. There is no other hand quite like mine in the world. My hand is like . . .

Edit Your Work

A. **Revise** your first **draft**, using the content checklist on page 136.

B. There are several kinds of comparisons that we can use to improve our writing. A **simile** is a comparison that begins with *like* or *as*. A simile compares things that seem very different, but are alike in some way. Read the following poem. The poet has used several similes to describe the base stealer. Can you find them?

> **The Base Stealer** by Robert Francis
> Poised between going on and back, pulled
> Both ways taut like a tightrope-walker,
> Fingertips pointing the opposites,
> Now bounding tiptoes like a dropped ball
> Or a kid skipping rope, come on, come on,
> Running a scattering of steps sidewise,
> How he teeters, skitters, tingles, teases.
> Taunts them, hovers like an ecstatic bird,
> He's only flirting, crowd him, crowd him,
> Delicate, delicate, delicate, delicate — now!

Look at the paragraph describing your hand. Did you use any similes? A **metaphor** also compares things that seem very different, but are alike in some way. Reread the poem "What Is This?" on page 34. What metaphor is used to describe the subway? List the different ways the poet has made the comparison. Read your paragraph once more to see if you can improve your use of similes and metaphors. Then write your final draft for your teacher to read.

Use The Language Arts

Write riddles for objects in your classroom. Write them in cutout shapes and display them around the room for others to read. The riddles on page 35 may give you some ideas.

You may wish to put some of your writing in your **writing folder**.

Can you say, "Tom threw Tim three thumbtacks?"
Can you say it three times? Words are made up of
sounds, rhythms, spellings, and shapes. This means
that words can be played with — arranged, turned
around, and repeated. It is fun to create tongue
twisters for your friends to try and say.

from The biggest tongue twister book in the world
by Gyles Brandreth

Swim, Sam, swim,
Show them you're a swimmer!
Six sharp sharks seek small snacks,
So swim, Sam, swim!

A clipper ship shipped several clipped sheep.
Were these clipped sheep the clipper ship's sheep?
Or just clipped sheep shipped on a clipper's ship!

Cliff Cross crossed the criss-cross crossing.
The criss-cross crossing Cliff Cross crossed.
When Cliff Cross crossed the criss-cross crossing,
Where's the criss-cross crossing Cliff Cross crossed?

A tree toad loved a she-toad
  That lived up in a tree.
She was a three-toed tree toad.
  But a two-toed toad was he.
The two-toed toad tried to win
  The she-toad's friendly nod.
For the two-toed toad loved the ground
  On which the three-toed toad trod.
But no matter how the two-toed tree toad tried
  He could not please her whim.
In her tree-toad bower,
  With her three-toed power,
The she-toad vetoed him.

---

1. With a partner, practise saying one of the tongue twisters out loud.
2. Try saying a tongue twister faster and faster. How many times can you repeat it without a mistake?
3. In groups, act out a tongue twister. How will you divide the lines?
4. Try to find examples of tongue twisters in newspaper headlines and advertisements.

THE WRITING WORKSHOP

Get Ready

Why are tongue twisters difficult to read orally? Is *tongue twister* a good name for this kind of poem? Why?

In a tongue twister, one or more sounds are repeated. Tongue twisters use a great deal of alliteration. **Alliteration** occurs when two or more words in a line begin with the same sound. Find three examples of alliteration in the poem "A Tree-Toad Loved a She-Toad" on page 39.

Start Writing

Write two tongue twisters to publish in a class book.

A. Use "Swim, Sam, Swim" on page 38 as a pattern. Write a poem about one of these:
- Teresa running from ten tigers
- Angelo ambling after an ape
- Flora fleeing from four foxes
- Evelyn elevating eleven elephants

B. Write a second tongue twister on whatever topic you like. Use one of these first lines if you like:
- A fat fish loved a flatfish.
- Karen cuddles Kevin's kitten.

Edit Your Work

A. **Revise** your work, using the content checklist on page 136.

B. In groups of four, edit your work. First, read your tongue twisters to your group for enjoyment. Next, each member of the group will select one of these editing jobs:
1) Edit for spelling.
2) Edit for capital letters and punctuation.
3) Edit to see if action words and describing words are

the best ones that could be used.

4) Edit to suggest other examples of alliteration that could be used.

Your paper will be read and edited by each member of the group. Look at the changes they recommend. Rewrite your tongue twisters making any changes you think will improve your work.

C. Tongue twisters often use homophones. A **homophone** is a word that sounds the same as another word, but has a different meaning and usually a different spelling. What is the homophone in this well-known tongue twister?

How much wood would a woodchuck chuck
If a woodchuck could chuck wood?
He'd chuck all the wood that a woodchuck could
If a woodchuck could chuck wood.

Write one-sentence tongue twisters, using the homophones below:
- dear — deer
- here — hear
- seen — scene
- there — they're — their

Can you use homophones in clever ways to make your tongue twisters even more interesting?

Use The Language Arts

A. Organize your tongue twisters into a class book. Two students can take care of this. They will select a title and design a cover. Also, take turns recording your tongue twisters on a cassette tape. These should be in the same order as the tongue twisters in the class book so that the book and the tape can be enjoyed together.

B. In groups of four, prepare two or three tongue twisters. Your class could then visit another class and present a "tongue twisting show." Perhaps your principal will let you present some of your tongue twisters over the P.A. system.

PERSUASION

Are you skilled at convincing your friends to do things you want them to do? There are many methods we can use for persuasion, from pleading with to bribing another person. In this letter a young girl writes to her new pan pal in Alaska. She tries to persuade her pen pal to come and visit her.

from Julie of the wolves
by Jean Craighead George

Hello, my new friend,

I am Amy Pollock and I have blue eyes and brown hair. Next month I will be twelve years old, and I hope I'll be five feet (1.5 m) tall by then. I have a quarter of an inch (.6 cm) to go. I wear a size nine dress and a size six shoe, which my mother finds embarrassingly big. Frankly, I like my big feet. They get me up and down the steep hills of San Francisco and shoot me through the water like a frog when I swim. I am in the eighth grade and am studying French. I hate it, but would like to learn Inuit. My father goes to Alaska often and he has taught me a few words. They are pretty words that sound like bells, but I can't spell them. Can you? How do you spell the word for *daylight? Quag?*

I take dancing lessons, which I love, and I also like to play baseball with the kids that live on our hill. When I grow up I think I'll be a dancer, but it is an awful lot of work. One of the dancers at the San Francisco Opera House said so, so maybe I'll be a schoolteacher like my aunt and have the whole summer off.

Last month at school we saw your island on a television show. It was so beautiful, with the birds flying over it and the flowers blooming on its hills, that I wanted to write to someone who lives there, a girl like me.

Here is a picture of my house. That is me standing on one foot on the patio wall. Please write soon.

Your new friend,
Amy

P.S. When are you coming to visit us in San Francisco?

---

1. What have you learned about the two pen pals?
2. Do you think a visit would be successful?
3. What techniques is Amy using to persuade her friend to visit?
4. What do we mean by "the art of persuasion?"
5. In your life, who is the person you have the most difficulty persuading?
6. Why do some people need a lot of persuasion? Are they stubborn? Are they mean? Are they sometimes wise not to do what we say?

THE WRITING WORKSHOP

Get Ready

When you persuade people, you try to get them to agree with you about something you believe strongly. Just asking for things with a smile and a polite *please* does not always work. Often you need to give people good reasons if you want to persuade them to agree with you. To persuade people, it helps to organize and present your ideas in a convincing way. One way to learn how to do this is to practise writing paragraphs that persuade. Remember that a **paragraph** is a group of sentences about one subject or topic.

Start Writing

Write a paragraph to persuade someone to see things your way. Think of a person or a group of people you want to convince of something. You might want to persuade:
- a faraway friend to come and visit you
- the mayor to build a park in your neighbourhood
- your sister to give back the trucks you lent her two years ago
- your parents to let you get a part-time job

When you are finished, you can give your paragraph to the person or persons you are trying to persuade. Use this plan.

A. In point form, list:
- the person or persons you are trying to persuade
- the idea you are trying to get them to agree to
- five or six good reasons why they should agree with you

B. Begin your paragraph with a topic sentence. A **topic sentence** is the sentence that gives the main idea of the paragraph. The topic sentence is often the first sentence in a paragraph. Your topic sentence might be:
- There are many good reasons why we need a park in our neighbourhood.

- It will do you good to take guitar lessons with me.

C. In four or five sentences, develop your topic sentence. Write your good reasons in these sentences. Sentences that give details to support the main idea in a paragraph may be called **supporting sentences**. Make sure your supporting sentences are convincing.

D. Be sure to indent your paragraph. When we **indent** a paragraph, we begin the first line a short distance to the right of the margin. By indenting, we show the reader where paragraphs begin and end on a page.

Edit Your Work

A. Use the content checklist on page 136 to **revise** your work.

B. 1) In pairs, read your paragraphs. Are your topic sentences clear? Do they state the main idea you are trying to get across? Do the reasons you give in your supporting sentences sound convincing? Are there some weak reasons you should leave out? What other good reasons might you add? Make any changes that will make your paragraph more convincing.

   2) Give your paragraph to your teacher to read and edit.

   3) Rewrite your paragraph, and give it to the person or persons you are trying to persuade.

Use The Language Arts

A. Read your paragraph to the class. Do the other students agree with you? Answer any questions they may have.

B. Did you persuade the person or persons? Did they at least answer you in some way? If the answer is no, you may want to try again. You can write the person or persons a letter, or talk to them on the telephone.

STATING OPINIONS

FEELINGS

Why are some people afraid to share their feelings with others? We are all afraid of something; does that make us cowards? Sharing our fears may help make them disappear. When we write about our emotions, we are able to see them in black and white. Sometimes this helps us to understand our feelings and handle them better.

from **Robbers, bones and mean dogs**
by Barry and Velma Berkey

When I was ten we moved into a new house. When I went to bed in that house, I heard a lot of creaking noises. Every time I heard noises, it sounded like someone was walking in the house. That doesn't scare me any more. Even now I'm scared of roller coasters and high ferris wheels. But with most of my fears I get over them.

When I stand up and do something in front of new people I feel very unhappy and I don't feel like I am a person any more.

I fear wasps because I had a bad experience. When I was in grade four, we were playing outside for break. All of a sudden this wasp came and started buzzing around me. I flapped my hands at it and then ignored it. But all of a sudden, it came down on me and stung me. I let out a yell of agony. Everyone came over to see why I screamed. A teacher took me to the office to get it fixed up. Ever since then, if a wasp comes around, I go running.

Four years ago I fell four metres into a pit and lost my breath. My friend jumped in to help me out. When I finally caught my breath, I got out of the pit. I had cuts on my chin and above my right eye. He took me home and my mother patched me up. I was afraid of big holes after that and I still am.

When I was a baby, I was afraid of dogs. Also loud noises, especially thunder claps, scared me like mad when I was little. When I was five there were many things that scared me. I was afraid of being in the dark by myself. To help from being scared, I'd whistle or hum. When I was six I hated big dogs and loud noises. And I used to be scared to go to bed. I used to think there was a monster under my bed that would come up and eat me. But if I put my covers over me, I would be protected from the monster. I did that until I was nine.

---

1. What kinds of things are people afraid of in this selection?
2. Is it normal to have fears — like the writers of these paragraphs?
3. Writers often use *I* or *me* in personal stories. How does this help the reader?
4. What was your greatest fear as a young child?
5. What are your fears about the future? What are your parents' fears about you?
6. Do our fears change as we grow older?

THE WRITING WORKSHOP

Get Ready

A good way to understand our feelings is to talk or write about them. When our feelings are confused, it often helps to think them through by writing them down. If we do this, we usually feel better. Another good thing about writing down our feelings is that other people can then read them and find out what we are feeling. This way, they can understand us better.

Start Writing

The paragraphs on pages 46 and 47 talk about feelings of fear. We can write about any of our feelings. We can write about what makes us happy, sad, lonely, angry, or excited. Think about the feelings you have. Select one of these to write about. You might choose fear or loneliness. Pattern your paragraph after one of those on page 46 or 47.

On a piece of paper, write down the event that made you feel the way you did. Then list five or six important details that explain what happened, and why you felt as you did. You are going to write about these feelings in a paragraph. You will give your paragraph to your teacher and parents to read. Use your rough notes and this writing plan.

A. Write a topic sentence that tells the main idea of your paragraph.

B. Write five or six sentences that tell important details about what happened and why you feel the way you do.

C. Use the words *I* and *me* to keep your paragraph personal.

D. Be sure to indent your paragraph.

Edit Your Work

A. Read your paragraph again. Does your topic sentence tell

the main idea? Do all the other sentences tell something about the topic sentence?

B. Use the proofreading checklist on page 136 to edit your work with a partner.

C. A paragraph should stay on topic. A paragraph will **stay on topic** if all the ideas in it tell about the main idea. Read the paragraph below. There are two sentences that are not about the topic. Can you find them?

> After dinner last Sunday, I felt so lonely that my stomach hurt. I didn't cry, but I should have because then I might have felt better. Why did I feel so miserable? Our cat is black and white. I shouldn't have felt lonely because I had fun with my friends at the pool in the afternoon, and my Uncle Ed came over for dinner. But after the dishes were washed, everyone seemed to disappear. Uncle Ed went into the den to work with my Mom on some papers. Dad and my two sisters went downstairs to watch TV. I stood all alone on the porch and watched the big red sun disappear behind the distant trees. As the sun went down, it seemed to take my last bit of happiness with it. Just before dark, I couldn't stand it any more. I ran downstairs and sat beside my Dad on the couch. There is a green lamp beside the couch. He looked at me, smiled, and messed up my hair. I felt better then.

Read this paragraph again, leaving out the sentences that are not on topic. The paragraph should make better sense now.

Read your own paragraph again to make sure all of your sentences stay on topic.

D. Write your final draft. Give it to your teacher to read. Later, take it home and let your parents read it. Talk with them about it.

Use The Language Arts

In groups of four, read your paragraphs. Talk about them. Talk about how you feel at different times. When have you felt especially happy? Why? When have you felt especially angry? Why?

(Are you remembering to write in your journal?)

STATING OPINIONS

ESSAYS

In an essay, you can express your thoughts and feelings about a topic that interests you. Sometimes you can research information that will help you with your essay. Sometimes you can just write how you feel about your topic. An essay is personal; it is your ideas about a subject that interests you. Why is the writer writing about *nothing* in the following essay?

About nothing
by Jack Boulogne

If you think that there is nothing to be said about nothing, you are quite wrong. Nothing is full of surprises, when you start thinking about it. So, let's start thinking about NOTHING.

Imagine two boxes, identical in every way: the same colour, shape, size, and material sitting side by side. Both boxes are also empty (that is, they contain nothing), but one box has no oranges in it, and the other box has no apples in it. Would you say that both these boxes are still the same? Both contain nothing, but these two nothings are not the same nothing. One is the absence of apples; the other is the absence of oranges. So, we must say that there are many different kinds of nothing: no apples, no oranges, no goats, no houses, no ideas, no cars, etcetera. In fact, you might say, there is an infinite number of kinds of nothing.

Some people might think that all this is just a trick — a sort of joke. But, it is no joke! Consider, for example, what would happen if nothing did not exist.

This would have rather strange results. For example, would you be able to take the last apple out of a box of apples? No, you wouldn't because then the box would contain nothing, which is not allowed. But it is even worse than that. Think of what happens when you take one apple out of the box. What is in the space left by the apple? NOTHING! You're right! But again, this is not allowed because nothing is not supposed to exist. Therefore you cannot even take one apple out. It follows, if you think it out, that if nothing does not exist then something cannot exist either, because they depend on each other. If something cannot exist, then everything becomes nothing. This is an example of what philosophers call a PARADOX. Paradoxes are very hard to solve.

In mathematics, the importance of nothing is recognized by giving it a name: in English this is *zero*. Zero is the number of things in a collection that contains nothing. There are zero oranges in an empty box and also zero apples, of course. Our system of numbers depends on using zero, and without zero it wouldn't work at all.

So, you see, there IS a great deal to be said about nothing, and nothing is very important. Without nothing, something could not exist, in which case IT would be nothing. All this proves that nothing cannot NOT EXIST.

---

1. Why can so much be said about nothing?
2. Why do you think the author chose this particular topic to write about?
3. Who is the author writing *to* in this essay?
4. Do you prefer non-fiction essays or fiction stories? Could an essay ever be part of a novel?
5. When children are asked, "What are you doing?" and they reply, "Nothing," what do they mean? Do you ever actually enjoy doing nothing?

THE WRITING WORKSHOP

Get Ready

Writing an essay helps you organize your thinking on a topic. It helps you understand the topic better. It also helps you sort out your feelings about the topic. When others read your essay, they come to know the topic better too. (As well, they get to know you better because they find out what you are interested in, what you believe in, and how you feel.

Start Writing

Write a personal essay on a topic that is important to you. In this essay, try to persuade your readers to think and believe as you do about your subject. Show them why you feel strongly about the topic. You are writing this essay for your teacher to read. Some of your classmates will read it as well. Use this plan.

A. First, select a topic. Select one that you personally believe in strongly. Here are some ideas.
- It is wrong to keep animals in zoos.
- It is important to go to church.
- People should be able to keep pets in apartment buildings.
- It is wrong to waste food with so many starving people in the world.
- We must do something to stop pollution.

B. Your essay will be four or five paragraphs long.

C. Write an outline of your essay in point form. You may want to do it this way.

First Paragraph — Introductory Paragraph
   In this paragraph, write two or three sentences. Your topic sentence should *state the main idea of your essay*. Your topic sentence might be: "Pollution is a serious problem that we must solve." The other sentences could tell why it is important to do something about the problem.

Second Paragraph — Supporting Paragraph

In this paragraph, define the problem. That is, tell *what the problem is.*
Example:
- Define what you mean by pollution.
- Give several examples of pollution.

Third Paragraph — Supporting Paragraph

In this paragraph, tell *why you are concerned* about the problem. Tell what will happen if something is not done.
Example: Tell what might happen to our land, water, air, animal life.

Fourth Paragraph — Supporting Paragraph

In this paragraph, tell *what can be done* to solve the problem.
Example: Tell what new laws could be made, how polluted areas could be cleaned up, and so on.

Fifth Paragraph — Closing Paragraph

In this paragraph, suggest to your readers *how they can help.* Also, you might conclude by telling them how the world will be a better place if the problem is solved.

D. From your outline, write your essay.

Edit Your Work

A. Revise your essay, using the content checklist on page 136.

B. Give the essay to your teacher to read.

Use The Language Arts

Present your essay as a speech. Use the essay outline you prepared, or make up a new outline. Know your speech well. Memorize important parts of it. Use your notes only when necessary. Look at your audience. Speak in a clear voice that is loud enough for all to hear.

Some stories are written to try to trick you. When writers create an endless story, they repeat part of the story again and again, but try to fool you into continuing to read it. Many endless stories are folktales, and have been passed on by storytellers for years.

The bear in the woods of New Brunswick
Traditional

Once a boy was taking a walk in the woods of New Brunswick when he happened to meet a bear. The bear snarled and said, "I'm going to eat you up."

But the boy said, "Stop! Before you devour me, let me tell you a story."

"I just *love* stories," said the bear. So the two of them sat down on a fallen log and the boy started telling his story.

> "Once upon a time," he said, "a boy was taking a walk in the woods of New Brunswick when he happened to meet a bear. The bear snarled and said, 'I'm going to eat you up.' But the boy said, 'Stop! Before you devour me, left me tell you a story.' 'I just love stories,' said the bear. So the two of them sat down on a fallen log and the boy started telling his story."

>> "Once upon a time," he said, "a boy was taking a walk in the woods of New Brunswick when he happened to meet a bear. The bear snarled and said, 'I'm going to eat you up.' But the boy said, 'Stop! Before you devour me, let me tell you a story.' 'I just *love* stories,' said the bear. So the two of them sat down on a fallen log and the boy started telling his story."

>>> "Once upon a time," he said, "a boy was taking a walk in the woods of New Brunswick when he happened to meet a bear. The bear snarled and said, 'I'm going to eat you up.' But the boy said, 'Stop! Before you devour me, let me tell you a story.' 'I just *love* stories,' said the bear. So the two of them sat down on a fallen log and the boy started telling his story."

Suddenly the bear yawned loudly, interrupting the boy. "It seems to be *such* a long story!" he said. "When will it ever end?"

"If I told you," answered the boy, "it would ruin the whole story."

"That means I can't eat you up yet," said the bear. "I never could stand to leave a story unfinished." He sat down to go on listening.

The boy continued with his tale. "Once upon a time," he said, "a boy was taking a walk in the woods of New Brunswick . . . ."

And so on . . . and on . . . and on . . . and on . . . until the bear fell fast asleep. He never did catch on that the story was endless.

As for the boy, he quietly stole away, leaving the bear snoring. His endless story had saved his life.

---

1. When did you first know this was an endless story?
2. What do you notice about the character of the bear in the story?
3. Can you think of another ending to this story?
4. Why do you think storytellers invented the endless story?

THE WRITING WORKSHOP

Get Ready

Did the endless story trick the bear? Did it trick you?

Study the pattern of this endless story.

1) The **story beginning** tells you who the story is about. It tells you where it takes place, and what problem is to be solved.

- Who is this story about?
- Where does it take place?
- What problem does the boy have to solve?

2) The boy decides to solve his problem by telling an endless story.

- Why is the story endless?
- Does the plan work? Why?

3) What do you think of the **story ending**? Is it effective? Why?

Start Writing

Write an endless story for other students to read. Use this plan if you wish:

1) story beginning — tells who, where, what the story is about

2) endless story told several times to solve the problem

3) paragraph explaining how the endless story solved the problem

4) story ending

Use your own story idea, or one of these:

- Alphonso is watching the Edmonton Eskimos play the Toronto Argonauts on TV. His father comes into the family room. "Why haven't you cleaned up your room?" his father asks. Alphonso says, "Wait a minute. Let me tell you a story before you make me go and clean my room."

- Marleen, Janet, and Marie are standing in front of a

huge abandoned farmhouse on a dark windy Hallowe'en night. Marie and Janet dare Marleen to go in and search the house to make sure it is safe for them to go inside too. Marleen says, "Wait a minute. Let me tell you a story before I go in."

Edit Your Work

A. **Revise** your story, using the content checklist on page 136.

B. In groups of four, take turns reading your endless stories. Then read them a second time, and suggest ways of making the stories better. Did you follow the writing plan?

C. A **personification** is a comparison. A writer uses personification when he or she gives an animal or an object human abilities. The writer compares an animal or an object to a human in some way. Here are some examples. What is the comparison in each?

1) The hungry lion laughed at the tourists trapped in their car.
2) The sun smiled on the children at the beach.
3) The leaves danced in the wind.

Is personification used in "The Bear in the Woods of New Brunswick?" How? Have you used any personification in your story. If not, can you find places where you can use personification to make your story more interesting?

Now write your final draft.

Use The Language Arts

A. Let's pretend that the bear in "The Bear in the Woods of New Brunswick" is not fooled by the endless story trick. Write a different ending to the story.

B. Publish a class book of endless stories to add to your library.

A funny story can cheer you up when you are feeling uphappy. Writers use strange characters, humorous situations, or interesting words to make you laugh. Does the title of the following story give you any clues about the humour in it?

How trouble made the monkey eat pepper

Traditional West Indian story retold by Rita Cox

Ma Minnie lived in a tiny village in Trinidad, on the Islands. All the children around knew Ma Minnie, for she made her living selling the most delicious cakes and sweets.

Once a week this old lady went to market to buy molasses for making her coconut cakes. One day she started out late. By the time she was on her way back home, the sun was high in the sky and she became hot and more tired than usual.

So there Ma Minnie was, walking through the tall trees with a gourd of molasses on her head. She stubbed her foot against a stone, and the gourd fell crashing to the ground with the molasses spreading out all over.

Poor Ma Minnie! She picked up a piece of the gourd to scoop up the thick, sweet syrup. She wailed: "Ah me, what trouble! Look at my trouble!" — all the while licking her fingers. Then she continued sadly: "I'll have to go right back to market. Ah me!"

A monkey sitting on a tree limb above observed what was going on. When Ma Minnie had left, he scurried down and tasted the molasses.

"If this is trouble, then trouble is sweet. I'd like to have some myself. I think I'll go into town and buy some."

So Brer Monkey dressed himself in his scissors-tail coat and his fine top hat, and he set out for the market. He stopped at the first shop. "I've come to buy some trouble."

Silence.

"Trouble? Do you know what trouble is?" asked the shopkeeper.

"Yes, man, I know what trouble is and I want to buy all you have."

"All right," replied the shopkeeper. "Remember, you asked for it," and he went to the back of the shop while his customers giggled.

The shopkeeper returned with a big bag. "Here is your trouble, sir. Now will you pay me, please?"

Brer Monkey paid the shopkeeper, took the bag and left.

At last he came to a clearing under some trees. He put his bag down, removed his hat, and licked his lips in anticipation. Then he sat down and untied the bag.

Out rushed three fierce, hungry dogs. Poor Brer Monkey! He rushed up the nearest tree to escape from the attackers, who stayed at the bottom barking and yelping.

The dogs stayed beneath the tree for a long time, and Brer Monkey grew hungrier and hungrier. The dogs didn't go away.

Finally, in desperation, Brer Monkey leaned over and picked a fruit from an overhanging branch and hungrily stuffed it into his mouth. How could he know it was a hot pepper tree?

Oh, did it burn! Oh, did it hurt! How Brer Monkey suffered!

At last, the dogs went away and Brer Monkey rushed down and threw himself, fine clothes and all, into a nearby stream.

And that is how trouble made the monkey eat pepper.

---

1. Why do writers sometimes use monkeys in funny stories?
2. Why do you laugh when people fall down in cartoons and in stories?
3. What things make you laugh when you read a funny story?

THE WRITING WORKSHOP

Get Ready

"How Trouble Made the Monkey Eat Pepper" is a funny story. The author uses many techniques of humour to make this story funny.

1) What strange characters does she use?

2) What humorous situations does she describe?

3) What interesting words made you laugh?

4) How does the way the monkey dresses make the story funny?

Talk about some TV programs or movies that are funny. What makes them funny?

Start Writing

You can write a funny story to share with your friends. Use these techniques of humorous writing to make your story funny.

1) Write about one or more strange or foolish characters.

2) Think of an unusual or foolish situation involving your character(s).

3) Decide how your characters get into this foolish situation.

4) Decide how they get out of it (if they do).

5) Have your characters dress in a funny way.

6) Exaggerate the actions of your characters to make them funny.

If you wish, use one of these ideas to build your funny story:

1) Two foolish painters are trying to paint the front of a store on a windy day. The sidewalk is crowded with busy shoppers.

2) Three silly skiers are trying to walk through a revolving door while wearing their skis.

Edit Your Work

A. **Revise** your story, using the content checklist on page 136.

B. In groups of four, read your funny stories. Talk about what makes each story funny. Use the ideas above.

C. **Synonyms** are words that are nearly the same in meaning. *Fall, tumble,* and *stumble* are synonyms. **Antonyms** are words that are opposite in meaning. *Laugh* and *cry* are antonyms. A **thesaurus** is a book that lists synonyms and antonyms of words. The words we use have a great deal to do with how funny our stories will be. *Stumble* may be a better word than *trip* to describe a funny episode about a clumsy painter falling over a can of paint. It is important to consider several synonyms before you decide on the best word for a particular sentence.

The emotions of characters go from one extreme to another in funny stories. It helps to be aware of antonyms. The smiling painter who is happy at last after several unsuccessful attempts may suddenly become a frowning or anxious looking painter when he drops his brush loaded with paint on the police officer's hat. Read your story again to see if you can improve your choice of words to make it more humorous. Use a thesaurus or a dictionary to help you find the best words possible.

Now write your final draft.

Use The Language Arts

A. Take the story from one of your favourite funny TV programs and write it as a humorous story to share with your class.

B. Prepare a class book of funny stories.

When writing in your journal, you can sometimes write about true to life, funny incidents.

Why do young children enjoy animal stories in which the animals behave like humans? When you write a story for primary children, you will be a Young Author. If you wish, you can have the animals in your story act and speak just like people. When you read the following story, you will see the combination of animal and human behaviour that the author uses to create the characters.

The special gift

from *George and Martha: tons of fun*
by James Marshall

It was George's birthday, and Martha
stopped by the bookshop to buy a gift.
"He loves to read," Martha told the
salesperson.

On the way to George's
    house,
Martha played a tricky
    game of
hopscotch.

George could hardly wait
    for his gift.
"I can't stand the suspense,"
    he said.
But when Martha went to
    look for George's
book, it wasn't there.
"I'm waiting," said George.
"What will I do?" said
    Martha to herself.
"I'm waiting," said George.

Martha quickly decided to
     give George
a photograph of herself.
"It's not much," she said.
When George saw Martha's
     picture,
he fell off his chair laughing.
"*Well!*" said Martha. "What's
     so funny?"

"This is the best gift I've
     ever received,"
said George.
"It *is?*" said Martha.
"Of course," said George.
     "It's wonderful to have
a friend who knows how to
     make you laugh."
Martha decided to swallow
     her pride.
She saw that the photograph
     was pretty funny
after all.

THE END

1. How do you know that George and Martha were friends?
2. Would you rather give a gift or receive one?
3. Why do family members and friends enjoy taking pictures of each other.
4. Read this story aloud in groups of three. One person can be the narrator, and the other two can be George and Martha.

THE WRITING WORKSHOP

Get Ready

Do you think younger boys and girls would enjoy the picture book on pages 62-64? What would they like about it?

Start Writing

You can write and illustrate a picture book. You can write it for younger boys and girls to enjoy. A **character description** is a group of sentences that can make a character real to your readers. A character description might tell these things about a person in a story:

- height, body build
- type of hair, face, and so on
- clothes they wear
- how they move

Read over the story outline below. You can write your picture book by completing this outline.

What Is the Problem, Andy Anderson?

page 1

This is Andy Anderson. This nice old man is sitting in Eaton's department store. He thinks he has a problem. You will learn about his problem when you read page 4. Don't read page 4 now. (Draw a picture of an unhappy Andy.)

page 2

This is Brenda. Brenda is . . . (Write a character description of Brenda and draw a picture of her.) Brenda is happy because she will be ten years old tomorrow.

page 3

This is Burt. Burt is . . . (Write a character description of Burt and draw a picture of him.) Burt is happy because he will be ten years old tomorrow.

page 4

Brenda and Burt are twins. They can hardly wait until tomorrow because they are going to a birthday party at their Grandpa's house. Andy Anderson is the twins' Grandpa. His problem is this. What should he get each of his grandchildren for their birthday?

page 5

All of a sudden Andy knows what to get for Brenda . . . (Tell what he gets Brenda, and give three reasons why it is a good gift for her. Draw a picture of the present.)

page 6

Andy is laughing. He is very happy. He doesn't have any problems now. He just thought of what Burt would like . . . (Tell what he gets Burt, and give three reasons why it is a good gift for him. Draw a picture of this present.)

page 7

Here are Brenda and Burt with Grandpa at their birthday party. They like the presents very much. Most of all, they love their Grandpa. They are happy just to be with him on their birthday. (Draw a picture of all three at the party.)

Edit Your Work

Describing words are words that tell about a person, a thing, a place, or an action. Review your character descriptions again. Have you used the best describing words you can think of? Make any change you think will improve your story.

Use The Language Arts

Read your picture book to one or more younger children. Make sure they can follow the pictures as you read the story.

SURVEYS

Have you ever seen people being interviewed at a shopping mall about their opinions on some important issue? Often information gathered by interviewing a number of people can be presented as a survey. Interviews conducted on paper are called *questionnaires*. Do you agree with the following survey?

Some favourite books

from Children's choices of Canadian books

Death over Montreal by Geoffrey Bilson

The other Elizabeth by Karleen Bradford

The bells on Finland Street by Lyn Cook

The mystery of Castle Hotel by Janice Cowan

The TV war and me by Sonia Craddock

You can pick me up at Peggy's Cove by Brian Doyle

Kap-Sung Ferris by Frances Duncan

The tin-lined trunk by Mary Hamilton

Frozen fire: a tale of courage by James Houston

Gold-fever trail: a Klondike adventure by Monica Hughes

The tomorrow city by Monica Hughes

This CAN'T be happening at Macdonald Hall! by Gordon Korman

White fang by Jack London

The twelve dancing princesses by Janet Lunn

The city underground by Suzanne Martel

Anne of Green Gables by Lucy Maud Montgomery

Owls in the family by Farley Mowat

Jacob Two-Two meets the Hooded Fang by Mordecai Richler

Amulets and arrowheads by Sheila Rolfe

King of the grizzlies by Ernest Thompson Seton

Underground to Canada by Barbara Smucker

On stage, please by Veronica Tennant

The hundred thousand dollar farm by Diana Walker

Murder on the Canadian by Eric Wilson

The wild Canadians by Chip Young

A boy at the Leafs' camp by Scott Young

---

1. Have you or your friends read any of these books?
2. Have a discussion: "Should Canadian children try to read Canadian books and watch Canadian television programs?"
3. How can computers help in taking a survey?
4. Is there such a thing as "a book for girls" or "a book for boys?" Should there be?
5. How can a person carrying out a survey try to make it fair and balanced?

THE WRITING WORKSHOP

Get Ready

By using a **questionnaire**, you can gather information from many people about important topics.

Read the sample questionnaire below. Do not complete it now.

TV-watching Questionnaire

Name _____ Age _____ Boy or Girl _____

1) Do you watch some TV almost every day? YES ____ NO ____
2) What is the average number of minutes a day you spend watching?
   ____ 0 - 5
   ____ 6 - 15
   ____ 16 - 30
   ____ 31 - 60
   ____ more than 60
3) What do you watch?

	NEVER	SELDOM	ONCE IN A WHILE	OFTEN
cartoons				
comedy shows				
detective shows				
game shows				
musical shows				
documentaries				
news				
sports reports				
other				

4) What do you like to watch the most?

_____

5) What do you like to watch the least?

_____

6) What are your main reasons for watching TV?

_____

_____

By using a questionnaire like this, you could gather a great deal of information about people's TV-watching habits. Your class may wish to make copies of the TV-watching

70

questionnaire. Each student can fill it out for himself or herself. (Please do not write in this book.)

Start Writing

With a group of four, you can write a questionnaire to gather information about people's reading habits. Each of you can give your questionnaire to four people outside of your class. You can ask them to read and fill it out. Use the questionnaire above as a guide if you like. What kinds of reading material will you ask about? You may wish to include some of the following: newspapers, comic books, magazines, novels, poetry books, science books, joke books, cookbooks, short stories.

Edit Your Work

A. Join with another group of four. Share your questionnaires. Go over them carefully to try to improve them. Use any good ideas the other group offers to make your questionnaire clearer and more complete.

B. Carefully print your questionnaire on a ditto master, or use some other method that will let you make copies. Make 21 copies. Give one copy to your teacher. Each group member will keep a copy. Each group member will also take four copies of the questionnaire to give to four people outside the class to read and fill in. Ask the people to return the completed questionnaires within two days.

Use The Language Arts

A. In your groups of four, read over the questionnaires that were returned. Talk about the answers. Compare them.

B. Use the information gathered from the questionnaires to write a group report.

NEWS REPORTS

Have you ever had your name mentioned in a news-paper report? Did the reporter get the facts correct? A news article begins with a headline that states the main idea. Then the important details follow. They answer the questions Who? When? Where? What? Why? and How?

from **The pushcart war**
by Jean Merrill

The Daffodil Massacre

The Pushcart War started on the afternoon of March 15, 1986, when a truck ran down a pushcart belonging to a flower peddler. Daffodils were scattered all over the street. The pushcart was flattened. The owner of the pushcart was pitched headfirst into a pickle barrel.

The owner of the cart was Morris the Florist. The driver of the truck was Mack, who at that time was employed by Mammoth Moving. Mack's full name was Albert P. Mack. But in most accounts of the Pushcart War, he is referred to simply as Mack.

It was near the corner of Sixth Avenue and 17th Street that the trouble occurred. Mack was trying to park his truck. He had a load of piano stools to deliver, and the space in which he was hoping to park was not quite big enough.

When Mack saw that he could not get his truck into the space by the curb, he yelled at Morris the Florist to move his pushcart. Morris' cart was parked just ahead of Mack.

Morris had been parked in this spot for half an hour, and

he was doing a good business. So he paid no attention to Mack.

Mack pounded on his horn.

Morris looked up then. "Why should I move?" Morris asked. "I'm in business here."

So when Mack yelled again, "Move!" Morris merely shrugged.

"Move yourself," he said, and went on talking with his customer.

"Look, I got to unload ninety dozen piano stools before five o'clock," Mack said.

"I got to sell two dozen bunches of daffodils," Morris replied. "Tomorrow they won't be so fresh."

"In about two minutes they won't be so fresh," Mack said.

Mack was annoyed. Like most truck drivers of the time, he was used to having his own way. Mammoth Moving was one of the biggest trucking firms in the city, and Mack did not like a pushcart peddler arguing with him.

When Mack saw that Morris was not going to move, he backed up his truck. Morris heard him gunning his engine, but did not look around. He supposed Mack was going to drive on down the block. But instead of that, Mack drove straight into the back of Morris' pushcart. Daffodils were flung for thirty metres. Morris himself, as we have said, was knocked into a pickle barrel. This was the event that we now know as the Daffodil Massacre.

---

1. Summarize the news report that you have just read.
2. This is a fictional news report from the novel *The Pushcart War*. How does the author make it seem real?
3. How does interviewing a person involved in the event make the report better?
4. Collect several reports of an event that interests your class. How are the reports the same? How are they different?

THE WRITING WORKSHOP

Get Ready

Newspapers often give us information in short, factual reports. These reports are about important and interesting people and events.

Eels helped over dam

TORONTO (CP) — More than 130 000 eels were able to go over a hydro dam in Cornwall with the help of a 500-foot (152-m) ladder built for them, Ontario conservation officers say.

The 100-foot (30-m) Robert Saunders Dam had prevented the migration of eels into tributaries of the Great Lakes until the ladder of wooden troughs was set up to criss-cross the face of the dam 7 1/2 times, the Ontario ministry of natural resources said in a news release.

The ladder is believed to be the only one of its kind and the highest in the world. It was recently disconnected for the winter.

Cup berth up for grabs

QUESNEL (CP) — Quesnel Kangaroos meet Prince Rupert this weekend in a best-of-three semi-final series in the B.C. intermediate hockey playoffs for the Coy Cup title.

Quesnel is the defending B.C. champion and will play host to games Friday and Saturday nights, plus a third game Sunday if required.

The winner meets Chilliwack Blues in the B.C. final, beginning March 25 in Chilliwack.

A good news article usually gives information by answering most of the following questions.

- *Who* is involved?
- *What* happened? or *What* will happen?
- *Where* did it happen? or *Where* will it happen?
- *When* did it happen? or *When* will it happen?
- *Why* did it happen? or *Why* will it happen?
- *How* did it happen? or *How* will it happen?

Which of the six questions do each of the newspaper reports answer?

Start Writing

Write a news report to publish in a class newspaper. Write

about an event that you saw in person or on TV.

Here are some examples:

- The Edmonton Oilers defeat the Calgary Flames.
- The Montreal Expos defeat the New York Mets.
- Eleven-year-old student wins prize in contest.

As you write, remember these important facts:

- News reports should be short, clear, and accurate.
- News reports should answer all or most of the six questions of good reporting.

Edit Your Work

A. Read your article again to see that your facts are accurate and that you have answered the six questions of good reporting.

B. A **headline** is the title that is put on a newspaper report. Headlines should be short. They should tell what the story is about in an interesting way. One way to make headlines effective is to use expressive **action words** or **verbs**. Notice the expressive action words in these headlines:

Blue Jays wallop Yankees

Jet explodes in ball of flames

Rewrite the headlines below, using more expressive actions words:

Leafs defeat Boston

Train hits transport

Roof falls on firefighters

Now check the headline you wrote for your news report. Can you improve your headline by using a more expressive action word?

Use The Language Arts

Read the sports pages from one or more local newspapers. Clip the headlines you find most interesting. Make a display of these headlines. Be prepared to tell why you find each headline effective.

PROJECTS

What things in life would you like to know more about? After you have chosen a topic to research, you have to decide exactly what you want to find out. You can write down several questions that you would like to have answered. Next, you must locate information — in books, articles, filmstrips, and so on. Then you must decide how you will write up the information you have found.

Dragons
by Barbara Ninde Byfield

Common physical characteristics:

corrosive and venomous spittle,
which drips from a forked tongue
  clanging scales
  fire-breathing nostrils
  lidless eyes
  terrible jaws, with many rows of teeth
  scalding blood
  a soft spot in belly or head
  lashing tail, with stinger on the end

Common behavioural characteristics:

Dragons drag; they are lazy, sluggish, and prefer to live on
their reputations.
  If guarding a treasure, they do so by sleeping on it.
  If they live in a lake, the water will seethe and steam.
  Like Nobility, they take place names for their own.

Considering that the business of Dragons is terrifying, ravishing, destroying, and scouring, they are remarkably careless about it. They do very little actual work. Only occasionally does a Dragon go rampaging, and then indeed an entire countryside can be laid to waste.

Dragons always appear at the last possible minute.

All of the above is fortunate, for it makes them extremely easy to avoid. (Have you ever seen a Dragon?) If you are out Questing, they are extremely easy to find and slay. (Have you ever met anyone who, having come to grips with a Dragon, didn't kill it?).

When entering battle with a Dragon, start from a distance. Dash straight and sure at his head, having first drawn your sword. The Dragon will parry with a limb or tail and your blade will clang off his scales; the sound is horrifying and well worth hearing. Several more such attempts, as many as please the bystanders, are necessary. When the Dragon gets you in his coils, begin seeking the soft spot on his belly or head. When it is found, you may kill him at your leisure.

It is well to step back after delivering the death blow. Dragons die hard, slowly, painfully, and if possible with one last act of vengeance. They need a great deal of room for their death throes and the accompanying lashings and thrashings, bellowings, and roarings.

Disposal of the body may take care of itself, for some Dragons when slain dry up into a handful of dust, or melt into a large grease spot, or evaporate. If not, they decompose very quickly and completely. A tooth or two makes a welcome souvenir to take to an Alchemist. A drop or two of Dragon's blood gives courage, invulnerability, and magical understandings.

---

1. What did you learn about dragons from this research project?
2. Do you think dragons ever actually lived? Where did the information in this research project come from?
3. How can you decide on a topic for a project?
4. Could you write a project that grade one children would enjoy reading?

THE WRITING WORKSHOP

Get Ready

You can research information about a topic. Then you can write down the facts you have learned. When you do this, you are preparing a **research report**. A research report can tell many people what you have learned about a topic.

Start Writing

You can write a research report about a mysterious creature. Other students will read your report. Follow the steps of the S.C.O.P.E. plan given below to write a good research report.

1) S is for **select** a topic. Some possible mysterious creatures to research are:

- The Sasquatch
- The Unicorn
- The Loch Ness Monster
- The Giant Squid

2) C is for **collect** information. Now that you have selected your topic, write down five or six questions that you want your report to answer. These questions will help you decide what information you need to research. Use these guides to good research.

- An **encyclopedia** is a collection of books that contain information about many topics. Try to find your topic there.
- A **subject card catalogue** in the library can tell you where to find information about your topic. If you need to, ask a librarian for help.
- An **index** of a book will tell you what pages give information about your topic. The index is usually found at the back of the book. It lists topics in alphabetical order.

Using your two or three (or more) reference books, make an **outline** of the information for your report. You can do this by writing down the questions you want your report to answer. Leave space between questions. As you collect information to answer questions, write it in point form under the questions.

3) O is for **organize** the information you have collected. Organize your information by using this plan:

Paragraph 1 — Introduction or Opening

In this paragraph, tell what your report is about. You may want to ask your readers one or more questions about your topic to raise their interest. You can answer these questions later in your report.

Paragraph 2 — First Question

Answer the first question. Suppose your first question is "What is a Sasquatch?" You could write a topic sentence giving the main idea of your answer. Then you could write one to three sentences giving more details and supporting the topic sentence.

Paragraphs 3, 4, and 5 — One for each of the other questions you are answering.

Paragraphs 6 — Conclusion or Ending

To conclude, write one or two sentences in which you make some summarizing comments about your topic.

4) P is for **present** your report. You can do this by reading it and talking about it with a group of students. They can read it for themselves as well.

5) E is for **evaluate** your report. You will do this with a partner in the Edit Your Work section. Your teacher can also evaluate your report.

Edit Your Work

Share your report with a partner. Edit each other's work by going through the S.C.O.P.E. plan again. Make any necessary changes and write your second draft.

Use The Language Arts

Make some drawings, paintings, or other illustrations to go with your report.

MAPS AND ATLASES

Most people dream of travelling to faraway spots for holidays or adventures. It is fun to look up places in an atlas, and then read about them. The following description and map are about an imaginary place that Robert Louis Stevenson told of in his book *Treasure Island*.

from The dictionary of imaginary places
by Alberto Manguel and Gianni Guadalupi

Treasure island, some sixteen kilometres long and eight kilometres wide, off the coast of Mexico. Near its southern point lies a cluster of rocks known as Skeleton Island; the two are joined by a spit of sand at low tide. There are three hills on Treasure Island, running north to south in a row. They are known as Foremast Hill, Mazenmast Hill, and Main Mast or Spyeglass Hill. The latter is the highest, rising sixty to ninety metres above the others. A natural harbour, known as Captain Kidd's Anchorage, lies on the south coast. It is almost landlocked, with trees coming right down to the highwater mark. Two swampy streams or rivers empty into this sheltered bay; the foliage around their mouths has an almost poisonously bright appearance.

The only buildings on Treasure Island are a stockade and a loghouse of pine hidden in the woods near the southern anchorage. Built over a freshwater spring on a knoll, the stockade can hold about forty people. It was obviously designed for defensive purposes and is pierced with loopholes for muskets on every side.

Much of the island is covered in grey woods, with occasional clumps of taller trees of the pine family. Low evergreen oaks are common. Flowering shrubs and clove trees are found on the rising ground above Captain Kidd's Anchorage. The fauna of the island has not been studied in any detail, although sea-lions are seen on the coast.

The island was first charted in 1754 by Captain Flint, who chose it as the burial place for his famous treasure.

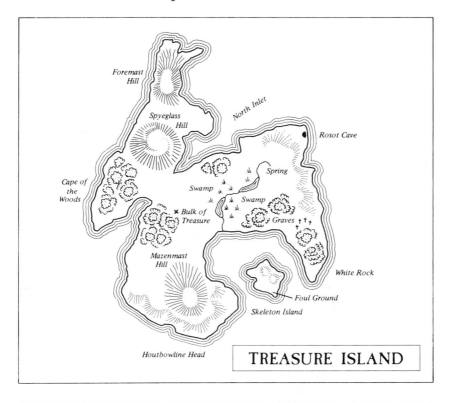

TREASURE ISLAND

1. Why do you think there are so many stories about treasure maps?
2. What words in the map and the description make you think of pirates?
3. Why do you think a stockade was built on the island?
4. Is this island near the "Bermuda Triangle?" Try to find out.
5. What other imaginary places would you enjoy seeing maps of?

THE WRITING WORKSHOP

Get Ready

There are many kinds of maps. There are imaginary ones such as the Treasure Island map. However, most maps are about real places. The map below is a neighbourhood map. A **map legend** is a list of the symbols used on the map. Use the symbols in the legend to help you read the map.

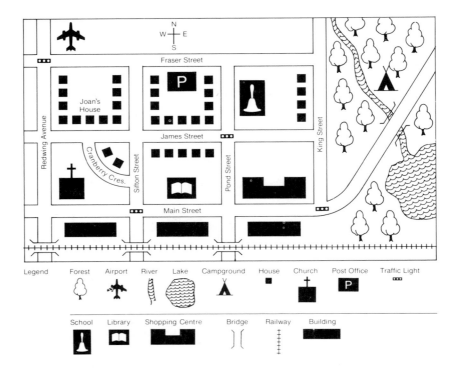

- What street would you take to go out into the forest?
- What street is the school on?
- How would Joan get to school from her house?
- How would Joan get to the library from her house?

Start Writing

Make a map of your neighbourhood to display in the hall and to show your family. Use this plan.

A. Decide on how much of your neighbourhood you are going to map.

B. Draw the blocks and streets and put their names on them.

C. Make a list of all the types of buildings and places in your neighbourhood. Decide on a symbol for each. Use the symbols from the map above if you wish.

D. Now mark your home on the map. Mark as many other buildings and places as you can remember.

E. Take a walk around your neighbourhood to fill in the buildings and places you were unsure of.

(The plan given above is for students who live in a city, town, or village. How will you change it if you live in the country? For example, maybe you will draw country roads instead of streets. Maybe your map will take in a larger area.)

Edit Your Work

A. Work with someone who lives close to you. He or she will probably have made a map of a similar area. Talk about the map legends you have used, and study your maps. Talk about them. Help each other make your maps more complete and accurate.

B. Make a final draft of your map.

C. Display your map in the classroom or in the hall.

D. Later, you can take your map home to share with your family.

Use The Language Arts

Make up an oral report about your neighbourhood. Instead of notes, maybe you can use your map as a reference when you speak.

WRITING POETRY

LISTS

There are many ways to list your feelings and ideas about a topic. By placing words on a page in interesting ways, you create patterns that have the power of a poem. Your poem can be a list of names of things, or details about a topic. Notice the interesting patterns in the following list poems.

Grocery list
by William Cole

When I was feeling strange one day,
* I made up a grocery list;*
I tried to get everything in it;
* Is there anything I've missed?*

One bunch of melons, one ear of clams,
One leg of prunes, a hand of hams;
A cube of corn, a sheaf of tomatoes,
An ear of lettuce, a jug of potatoes;
A clove of turnip, a chunk of beans,
 A tube of bananas, two metres of sardines;
  A sprig of eels, a sack of cheese,
  A grain of herring, a head of peas;
   A stalk of butter, a bottle of beef,
   A slice of rice, an asparagus leaf;
    A piece of soup, a Brussels sprout,
    And half a bar of sauerkraut.

I always like summer
by Nikki Giovanni

I always like summer
best
you can eat fresh corn
from daddy's garden
and okra
and greens
and cabbage
and lots of
barbecue
and buttermilk
and homemade ice cream
at the church picnic
and listen to
gospel music
outside
at the church
homecoming
and go to the mountains with
your grandmother
and go barefooted
and be warm
all the time
not only when you go to bed
and sleep

Fauna Canadiana
by Meguido Zola

Bison, badger, big brown bear,
Beaver, otter, varying hare;
Swift fox, striped skunk, star-nosed mole,
Chipmunk, chuck, and creeping vole;
Marmot, musk-ox, mountain goat,
Sea-mink, squirrel, fur seal, stoat;
'Possum, porpoise, pigmy-shrew,
Cuddle
Snuggle
Nuzzle
You!

---

1. Why do you think the poets wrote these poems?
2. Try chanting the poems aloud in groups. How many different ways can you think of to do this?
3. Use the table of contents or the index of a book to make a list poem. You could also use a restaurant menu to write a list poem.
4. Try to think of different ways of listing items; for example, by size.
5. Make up a list poem about a topic by having everyone in the class contribute one line.

THE WRITING WORKSHOP

Get Ready

Which list poem on pages 84-85 did you enjoy most? Why? Which poem is funniest?

Start Writing

Write your own collection of list poems. Write several different kinds. Later, you can publish a book of list poems with three other students.

Poem 1 — What Is It Poem

orange	green
crackling	croaking
smoky	slimy
warm	frogs
fire	

In this kind of list poem, you list several **describing words** that tell about a subject. The subject is revealed in the last word of the poem. The describing words should appeal to as many of the five senses as possible — sight, sound, smell, touch, taste. Read the two What Is It poems again. How did both poems follow the pattern? Now write your own What Is It Poem. Use any topic you wish, or try one of these.

Jell-O   dog   jet

Poem 2 — Three-Word List Poem

Read these poems.

spiders	beavers	cars
spin	bite	collide
speedily	busily	carelessly

Can you see the pattern in this form of list poem?
Subject (noun) xxxxxxxxxx
Action Word (verb) xxxxxxxxxx
Describing Word (adverb) xxxxxxxxx

Notice that each of the three words begins with the same sound. This is called **alliteration**.

Write two Three-Word List Poems. Use any subject you like, or consider these:

trucks   sharks   cats   brothers   cookies

Poem 3 — Sound List Poems

Some poems use words that imitate sounds. This is called **onomatopoeia**. Which words in the list poems below imitate sounds?

The sound of waves is: The church bell:

splash   clangs
lap   bangs
slap   dings
crash   rings
murmur   sings
roar

Write one Sound List Poem using the pattern above. Use any topic you wish, or try one of these:

rain   cannon   traffic   budgie bird

Edit Your Work

Revise your poems, using the content checklist on page 136.

Use The Language Arts

In a group of four, publish your own book of list poems. Your book can have the following parts:

front cover
table of contents
Chapter One — What Is It Poems
Chapter Two — Three-Word List Poems
Chapter Three — Sound List Poems
back cover

WRITING POETRY

SHAPE POETRY

A shape poem has the words arranged to show the topic in a way that can be seen. The shape in which the words are arranged, and the words themselves, combine to create the poem. It is fun to create shape poems for different topics.

Jellyfish
by Patrick Lashmar

Cats
by Cheryl MacDonald

```
  C C C
C
C
C
  C C C   urled up on a chair

    A
   A A
  A   A
 A A A A
A        A   nd purring

T T T T T
    T
    T
    T
    T    ill they fall asleep and dream of

   S S S
  S
 S
   S
       S
       S
S S S    omething special.
```

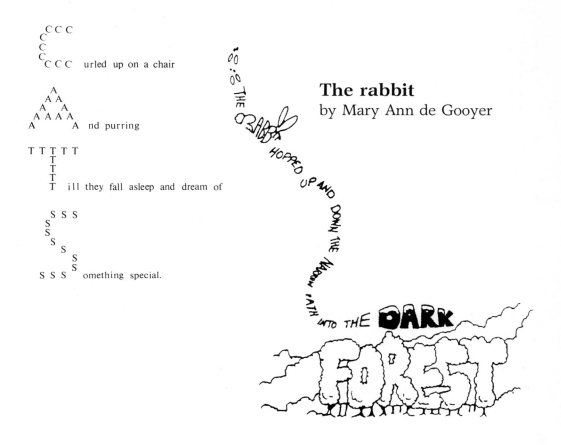

The rabbit
by Mary Ann de Gooyer

---

1. How could you say these poems aloud and yet help your listeners to see the shapes?
2. Can you make new shape poems, using the same words but different shapes?
3. Try rewriting the poems using typewriters or computers.
4. Could you use a shape poem to create a mobile? Try it with one of the poems above.
5. In groups, create shape poems using words from a newspaper.
6. Try to collect shape jokes, riddles, and poems from sources such as *Mad* magazine.

THE WRITING WORKSHOP

Get Ready

Look at the poem "The Rabbit" on page 89. Read it, trying not to pay attention to the shapes of the words. Read it again. This time, pay close attention to the shapes of the words. Look especially at the words *dark* and *forest*. How do the shapes of the words make this poem more interesting?

Start Writing

Write two shape poems. Later, you can use magic markers or crayons to print these poems on art paper. The shape poem you think is your better one can then be displayed in the hall for everyone to read.

Poem One

Read "The Rabbit" again. Use it as a model to write your first shape poem. Think of an animal, fish, or bird that is moving to some favourite place.
Examples:
A fish swimming in under a dark log.
A hawk flying to its nest on the side of the mountain.

Remember to write your words in a way that makes the meaning of your poem clear.

Poem Two

Now use "Jellyfish" on page 88 as a model. Look at the **action words** the poet used to describe the movements and actions of the jellyfish. Action words tell what a person or thing does. They may also be called **verbs**. Think of an animal, bird, or fish that moves in interesting ways. Think of effective verbs that tell how this creature moves. You may want to consider one of these subjects:

starfish   octopus   giraffe   spider   fly

Be sure to organize your words so that the shape of the completed poem is something like the creature you are describing.

Edit Your Work

A. With a partner share your poems. Talk about how the shapes of the poems make them more enjoyable and more interesting.

B. With your partner edit your work, using the proofreading checklist on page 136.

C. Talk with your partner about the action words used in poem two. Can you think of more interesting adjectives and verbs? Use a thesaurus or a dictionary to find synonyms that might be more effective.

Use The Language Arts

Select what you think is your better shape poem from the two you have written. Think about ways of printing this poem, using different art ideas. You may want to use markers and different shapes of paper. You may want to make your poem into a mobile. Now give your shape poem to your teacher to be displayed in the hall.

Select one or more of your shape poems to keep in your **writing folder**.

Many people write poetry in their journals. Are you remembering to write in the journal that you started in the Sharing Experiences section? Why not try to include some poetry?

WRITING POETRY

CINQUAINS

A cinquain (SANG-kane) is a shape poem composed of five lines. Each line has a special purpose. You can have fun playing with words and arranging them into cinquains.

Astronaut
Brave, daring
Excited, awed, mystified
A modern day explorer
Astronaut

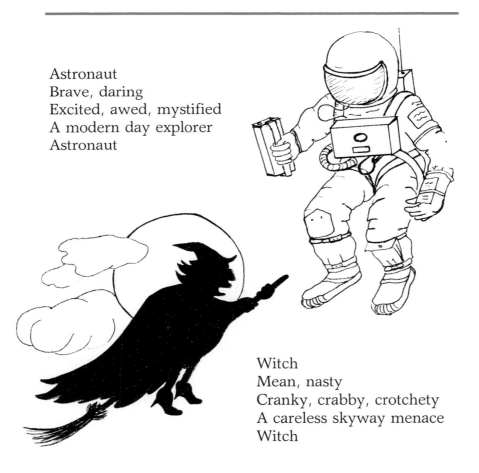

Witch
Mean, nasty
Cranky, crabby, crotchety
A careless skyway menace
Witch

Poem
Ringing, singing
Tender, touching, strong
Tugging at my heart
Poem

Birds
Plump, feathery
Flying, flitting, fluttering
Chattering on chimney tops
Birds

1. Read these cinquains aloud in groups.
2. What kinds of topics are most suitable for cinquains?
3. Select a newspaper story. Working with the ideas in the article, create a cinquain.
4. Choose a paragraph from a story that you are reading. Turn the ideas into a cinquain.

THE WRITING WORKSHOP

Get Ready

The poems on pages 92 and 93 use a limited number of words to describe something. Poets writing cinquain poems must be thoughtful about the words they select. They use few words to create an interesting picture.

Start Writing

Write three cinquain poems to share with someone in your family. To write a cinquain, you must know the pattern it follows. Use the questions below to help you discover the pattern for writing a cinquain poem. (Look at the poems on pages 92 and 93.)

A. How many lines are in each poem?
B. How many words are in line one? What does line one tell you?
C. How many words are in line two? What do they do?
D. How many words are in line three? What do they do?
E. How many words are in line four? What does line four tell you about the subject?
F. How many words are in line five? How is it related to line one? How well did you note the pattern?

    A **cinquain** is a five-line poem. Each line has a special purpose:
1st line — one word giving the subject
2nd line — two describing words telling about the subject
3rd line — three describing words telling about the subject
4th line — four words telling something more about the subject
5th line — line one repeated
Now write your own cinquain poems.

Poem One
    Write a cinquain telling about a person.
Some examples are:

- an athlete, actor, or actress you like
- astronaut, witch, soldier, nurse, missionary

Poem Two

Write a cinquain telling about one of your favourite things.
Some examples are:
- your favourite food; for example, hamburger, lasagna
- your favourite sport; for example, football, street hockey

Poem Three

Write a cinquain telling about an idea or feeling. Some examples are:
- wisdom, beauty, fun, truth, mystery
- love, hate, fear, joy, jealousy

Edit Your Work

In pairs share your cinquain poems. Edit your poems. Make sure that:
- each cinquain follows the correct pattern
- you have used the best describing words you can think of

Use The Language Arts

Make a booklet of your poems to give to someone in your family. Use these steps:

1) Decide who will receive your booklet. This will help you decide how to write and illustrate your poems.

2) Fold a piece of paper in half to make four pages.
- On page one, print or write the title of your booklet along with your name.
- Print or write one cinquain on each of the other pages.
- Illustrate each page in your booklet to add to the meaning of your poems.

WRITING POETRY

LYRICS

The words for a song are called *lyrics*. You probably remember many songs from when you were very young: for example, "The farmer in the dell" or "London Bridge is falling down." The framework of a song is fun to work with. The familiar tune and language patterns can help you write your own lyrics.

Comin' down the chimney
Lyrics adapted by Raffi

Traditional tune:
She'll be comin'
round the mountain

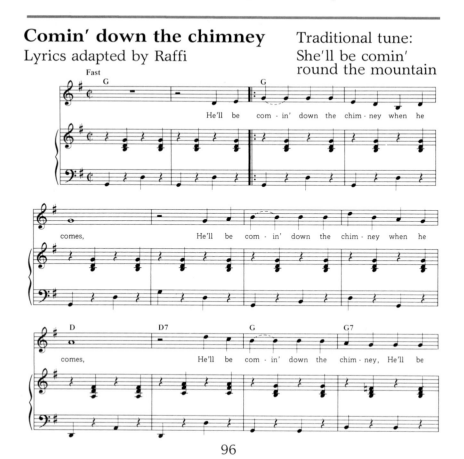

com - in' down the chim - ney, He'll be com - in' down the

chim - ney when he comes.   He'll be   comes.

Slowly

Com - in' down the chim - ney   when he comes.

2. He'll be bringin' lots of goodies . . .

3. He'll have all of his reindeer . . .

4. And he'll need some milk and cookies . . .

5. He'll be comin' down the chimney . . .

© 1980 Homeland Publishing (CAPAC)

1. Where do you think Canadian singer/songwriter Raffi got his idea for these song lyrics?
2. Create a new verse to go with this tune.
3. Select record albums with lyrics printed on them, and sing along with the records.
4. You may wish to design a new record jacket for one of your favourite records.
5. Choose a song that you enjoy and put it on an overhead projector for the class to sing. You can make up actions to go with the song or create a "homemade band" with instruments such as comb and paper.

THE WRITING WORKSHOP

Get Ready

The words to "Comin' Down the Chimney" are simple. The lines are repeated often. Boys and girls enjoy singing songs such as this. Why?

Start Writing

Some advertising jingles are very popular. Can you think of a jingle that you like? Can you sing it? It is fun to make up jingles to well known melodies. Sing the lyrics below to the tune of "My Bonnie Lies Over the Ocean."

A bottle of Sprite is so tasty,
A bottle of Sprite goes down right.
A bottle of Sprite is so tasty,
I drink it by day and by night.

Drink it,
Drink it.
I drink it by day and by night.

Use this melody or another well known melody to write some lyrics that advertise one of your favourite products. Melodies you might use would be: "Jingle Bells;" "Row, Row, Row Your Boat;" "Mary Had a Little Lamb."

Edit Your Work

A. In groups of four, read or sing lyrics. Speak or sing in a clear voice. Take turns reading or singing your lyrics as a group.

B. In groups of four, edit your lyrics. Help each other with the **rhythm. Rhythm** is something like beat in music. A line of poetry often has a set of number of strong and weak syllables that produce the "beat." Here is an example: Mý Bón-ńie liés ó-vér the ó-céan.

For the lyrics you have written, the melody sets the rhythm pattern. Each line must have enough words containing enough syllables so that, when you sing the words, they fit the melody. Say or sing each line of the lyrics. If a line has too many or too few syllables, rearrange it until it fits the rhythm pattern in the melody.

Use The Language Arts

A. In groups of four, in pairs, or by yourself, prepare to sing one or more of your lyrics for the class or for other classes. Use guitar or piano accompaniment if you wish.

B. Look for other songs by Raffi. What other Canadian singers do you enjoy listening to? If you like, bring recordings or tapes to school to share with other students. Make sure you handle them carefully, and take them home again when you are finished playing them.

Select one of your lyrics to keep in your **writing folder**.

Look over your journal. You see, you have written a long, interesting book all about you! Your book is not finished. Remember to continue to add to it.

FABLES

Have you ever read one of Aesop's fables, perhaps "The ant and the grasshopper" or "The dog and the bone?" Aesop's stories were written long ago. But writers still use the fable pattern today. A fable is a folktale that teaches a lesson. Often the author uses animals to represent humans. In this way, real people's feelings are protected. What is the lesson, or moral, in this modern fable?

The hippopotamus at dinner
by Arnold Lobel

The Hippopotamus went into a restaurant. He sat at his favourite table. "Waiter!" called the Hippopotamus. "I will have the bean soup, the Brussels sprouts, and the mashed potatoes. Please hurry, I am enormously hungry tonight!"

In a short while, the waiter returned with the order. The Hippopotamus glared down at his plate.

"Waiter," he said, "do you call this a meal? These portions are much too small. They would not satisfy a bird. I want a *bathtub* of bean soup, a *bucket* of Brussels sprouts, and a *mountain* of mashed potatoes. I tell you I have an APPETITE!"

The waiter went back into the kitchen. He returned carrying enough bean soup to fill a bathtub, enough Brussels sprouts to fill a bucket, and a mountain of mashed potatoes. In no time, the Hippopotamus had eaten every last morsel.

"Delicious!" said the Hippopotamus, as he dabbed his mouth with a napkin and prepared to leave.

To his surprise, he could not move. His stomach, which had grown considerably larger, was caught between the table and the chair. He pulled and tugged, but it was no use. He could not budge.

The hour grew late. The other customers in the restaurant finished their dinners and left. The cooks took off their aprons and put away their pots. The waiters cleared the dishes and turned out the lights. They all went home.

The Hippopotamus remained there, sitting forlornly at the table.

"Perhaps I should not have eaten quite so many Brussels sprouts," he said, as he gazed into the gloom of the darkened restaurant. Occasionally, he burped.

Too much of anything often leaves one with a feeling of regret.

---

1. What do you think the moral means?
2. Have you ever regretted overdoing something?
3. Could you eat: a bathtub of some food? a bucket of some food? a mountain of some food?
4. If the Hippo had read this story, do you think he would have understood the lesson?
5. Turn this fable into a monologue as spoken by the Hippo. Where will the setting be? What kind of voice will you use?

THE WRITING WORKSHOP

Get Ready

The **moral** in a fable is the lesson that it teaches. What is the moral in "The Hippopotamus at Dinner?" A fable, like other stories, has a plot. The **plot** in a story is the series of main events that take place in the story.

In a few sentences, summarize the plot in "The Hippopotamus at Dinner."

Start Writing

Write a fable for younger boys and girls to read. Your story can teach a lesson. Try to develop the main points of your plot well. Use this plan.

A. Decide on the moral you want your fable to teach. You could consider these:
- Too much of anything often leaves one with a feeling of regret.
- Don't try to be something you are not.
- Sometimes the weak can help the strong.
- Don't try to bite off more than you can chew.

B. Think of an animal to be your main character. Think of a story idea using this animal to teach your lesson. An elephant at a fast food restaurant might be an idea for the first example above. The moral in the second example could be developed from the idea of a turtle who wanted to fly.

C. Make your fable at least five paragraphs long. Make sure it has a definite beginning, middle, and end.

D. The first paragraph of your fable should introduce your main character or characters, and tell where the story is taking place. Be sure to make your animal characters act like people.

E. In the middle paragraphs, develop your story plot. Be sure each main event in the story leads up to the lesson or moral being presented.

F. In the last paragraph, tell the lesson learned by the main character or characters. In "The Hippopotamus at Dinner" the Hippo has eaten so much that he becomes stuck between the table and chair. What does he learn from this? What happens to your character or characters in the end? What lesson is learned from this? State your moral at the end. You may wish to state it on a separate line by itself.

G. Think of a good title for your fable.

Edit Your Work

A. **Revise** your fable, using these questions:

1) Is the moral presented clearly? Can I change my fable to make the moral clearer?

2) Do the animal characters I have developed stand for particular characteristics in people. For example, do I use a fox to represent proud, sly people? Do I use an elephant to represent strong, honest people?

3) Are the main events of the plot developed in an interesting way?

4) Does my fable have an opening paragraph, developing paragraphs, and a closing paragraph?

B. Answer the questions in the proofreading checklist on page 136. Write your second draft.

C. In groups of four, share your fables. Talk about the moral in each. What does the moral mean?

D. Give your fable to your teacher to read. Your teacher may make arrangements to have your fable read by younger boys and girls in another class.

Use The Language Arts

Most fables were told before they were written down in books. Read several fables. Select one that you particularly enjoy, and read it several times. Prepare to tell this fable to a group of students in your class.

FOLKTALES

Parents often tell children stories. Years later, the children tell *their* children, who tell *their* children, who tell *their* children . . . until the story becomes a folktale. Through storytelling, such tales are passed on from one generation to the next. Often a folktale teaches some kind of lesson.

The golden arm
Traditional

Turn out the lights before you tell this story, or tell it outdoors on a dark night when the moon doesn't shine . . .

There was an old woman in Antigonish, Nova Scotia who had a golden arm. The woman had lost her real arm in an accident.

When she died her arm was buried with her. But her husband wanted to get the golden arm. He knew that — if he did — he would be a wealthy man.

One dark night the husband, whose name was Marvin, stole into the Antigonish graveyard without anyone seeing him. Quickly he dug up his wife's body and took the golden arm.

As Marvin was hurrying home, the wind began to howl. It seemed to say, "Whooooo stole my golden arm? Whooooo stole my golden arm?"

Frightened, Marvin ran into his house. He locked all the doors and windows. Then he scurried upstairs, jumped into bed, and pulled the covers over his head.

"Whooooo stole my golden arm?" moaned the voice,

104

seeming to come nearer and nearer. "Whooooo stole my golden arm?"

By this time Marvin was shaking with fear. Under the covers he clutched the golden arm tightly to his chest.

Then, downstairs, he heard his front door slowly opening. Someone came inside. Footsteps creaked up the stairs . . . getting louder and louder and LOUDER.

At last Marvin's bedroom door opened. Footsteps creaked towards his bed. Suddenly the moaning voice whispered right in Marvin's ear. "Whooooo stole my golden arm. Whoooo? Whoooo?"

Stop at this point in the story. Then suddenly grab one of your listeners and shout, "YOU DID!"

---

1. Is there a lesson in this folktale?
2. What makes this story a good one to tell aloud?
3. How do you think this story began, many years ago?
4. Are there any stories that your family tells over and over? Perhaps they are about things that happened years ago, at a wedding or a birthday.
5. Now that we have television, will people still tell folktales?

THE WRITING WORKSHOP

Get Ready

When we are uncertain about what is going to happen in a story but want very much to find out, we say the story has **suspense**.

Where does the suspense begin in "The Golden Arm?" Does the suspense in this folktale make it more enjoyable? How?

In many stories, the main character must try to solve some kind of **problem**. What problem does Marvin have to try to solve in "The Golden Arm?" Do you think this is an interesting problem? Why? Does Marvin solve the problem?

Start Writing

Try writing a folktale to contribute to a class book. Before you begin, it is useful to know that a folktale often has these characteristics.
- It begins with "once upon a time."
- The main character has a clear problem to solve.
- A folktale often teaches a lesson of some kind.

To help plan your story, write down the answers to these questions in point form.
- What problem will your main character have?
- Where will your story take place?
- How will the problem in the story be solved?
- What lesson are you trying to teach your readers?

Now write your first draft.

Edit Your Work

A. **Revise** your folktale. Use these questions to help you.
- What is the problem to be solved?
- How is the problem solved?
- What is the lesson or moral in the story?

B. In your groups, use the editorial group checklist on page 136 to edit your folktales.

C. Revise and write your second draft. Give it to your teacher to read.

Use The Language Arts

A. Folktales are great for storytelling. They are good stories to present orally. Prepare to tell your folktale to the class by using these steps.

1) When you are getting ready to tell others a story, it is important to read it over again. Why do you think you should do this?

2) Find out where each event in your story begins and ends. Remember all the events in the order in which they occur.

3) Include interesting phrases and groups of words when you tell your story.

4) Tell the story to yourself in your own words. How can you help yourself remember all the story parts?

5) Practise telling the story to someone else before you tell it to your audience.

6) Be sure everyone in your audience is listening before you begin your story. How can you make sure your audience will keep on listening?

- Can you use your voice to help your audience hear what is happening in the story?
- Can you use your face, hands, and body to help your audience see what is happening?

B. Take turns taping your folktales. Other students can listen to your folktale later in the listening centre.

C. In a group prepare a short dramatization of a folktale to present to your class.

You may wish to keep your folktale in your **writing folder**.

GHOST STORIES

There are many tales of ghosts who wander the earth, either because they are being punished, or because they are searching for something. In such stories, people are sometimes allowed to actually see the ghosts. Ghost stories are passed on from one generation to another.

The ghost stallion
Blackfoot Indian story retold by Frances Fraser

This is a tale the old people tell around the tepee fire, when the stars are blown clean on a windy night, and the coyotes are howling on the plains around Buffalo Lake, Alberta. And when, sometimes, over the wind comes clearly the sound of running horses, their hearers move a little closer to one another — and pile more wood on the fire.

This is a story from a long time ago, say the Old Ones. What the man's name was, no one knows now, and so they call him "The Traveller."

Long ago, The Traveller was a wealthy chief. A warrior in his young days, he had taken many scalps, many horses, many another trophy of value. And he had increased his possessions by hard dealings with those less fortunate, and by gambling with younger men who were no match for his cunning.

He was not loved by his fellow tribespeople — though they admired his bravery — for in times of hardship, when other chiefs shared freely whatever they had, he drove hard bargains, and generally prospered from the ills of others. His wives he had abused till their parents took them away; his children hated him and he had no love for them.

There was only one thing he cared for — his horses. They were fine horses, beautiful horses, for he kept only the best; and when a young warrior returned from a raid with a particularly good horse, The Traveller never rested until (whether by fair means or not) he had it in his possession.

At night, when the dance drum was brought out, and the other Indians gathered round it, The Traveller went alone to the place where his horses were picketed, to gloat over his treasures. He loved them. But he loved only the ones that were young, and handsome, and healthy; a horse that was old, or sick, or injured received only abuse.

One morning, when he went to the little valley in which his horses were kept, he found in the herd an ugly white stallion. He was old, with crooked legs, and a matted coat, thin, and tired-looking.

The Traveller flew into a rage. He took his rawhide rope, and caught the poor old horse. Then, with a club, he beat him unmercifully. When the animal fell to the ground, stunned, The Traveller broke his legs with the club, and left him to die. He returned to his lodge, feeling not the slightest remorse for his cruelty.

Later, deciding he might as well have the hide of the old horse, he returned to the place where he had left him. But to his surprise, the white stallion was gone.

That night, as The Traveller slept, he had a dream. The white stallion appeared to him, and slowly turned into a beautiful horse, shining white, with long mane and tail — a horse more lovely than any The Traveller had ever seen.

Then the Stallion spoke: "If you had treated me kindly," it said, "I would have brought you more horses. You were cruel to me, so I shall take away the horses you have!"

When The Traveller awoke, he found his horses were gone. All that day, he walked and searched, but when at nightfall he fell asleep exhausted, he had found no trace of them. In his dreams, the White Stallion came again, and said, "Do you wish to find your horses? They are north, by a lake. You will sleep twice before you come to it."

As soon as he awakened in the morning, The Traveller hastened northward. Two days' journey, and when he came to the lake there were no horses.

That night, the Ghost Stallion came again. "Do you wish to find your horses?" it said. "They are east, in some hills. There will be two sleeps before you come to the place."

When the sun had gone down on the third day, The Traveller had searched the hills, but had found no horses. And so it went; night after night the Stallion came to The Traveller, directing him to some distant spot, but he never found his horses. He grew thin and footsore. Sometimes he got a horse from some friendly camp, sometimes he stole one in the night. But always, before morning, would come a loud drumming of hoofs, the Ghost Stallion and his band would gallop by, and the horse of The Traveller would break its picket and go with them.

And never again did he have a horse; never again did he see his own lodge. And he wanders, over the prairies, even to this day, the old men say, still searching for his lost horses.

Sometimes, they say, on a windy autumn night when the stars shine very clearly, and the coyotes howl, above the wind you may hear a rush of running horses and the stumbling footsteps of an old man. And, if you are very unlucky, you may see the Stallion and his band — and The Traveller, still pursuing them, still trying to get back his beautiful horses.

---

1. Did The Traveller deserve what happened to him?
2. Why did the Blackfoot people tell this story? How do you think it got started?
3. Would you know this was a North American Indian story if you had not been told?
4. Why do children enjoy stories and films about horses?
5. What other stories have you heard about ghosts who must wander the earth forever? Plan a ghost story festival, with each group retelling a favourite tale.

THE WRITING WORKSHOP

Get Ready

Why do boys and girls enjoy listening to ghost stories late at night? Do people enjoy being frightened? Why is this? A good writer of ghost stories likes to create a mood that makes the audience wonder if ghosts really exist.

How has Frances Fraser created a scary mood in "The Ghost Stallion?" Does this make the story more believable? How?

In a ghost story, the main character often encounters a supernatural being of some kind. The problem the character often has to solve in a ghost story is how to escape from this supernatural creature. Another important element of every story is **conflict**. Conflict consists of the struggle the main character has with another person, animal, or force as he or she tries to solve the problem in the story. The conflict in "The Ghost Stallion" is between people and a supernatural force. It is between the evil Traveller and the Ghost Stallion. When the problem in the story is solved, the conflict is often resolved as well. Is the conflict in "The Ghost Stallion" ever resolved?

Start Writing

Write your story in a way that makes it seem as if it really happened. Your story can tell about a character who is trying to solve a problem he or she has with a supernatural force of some kind. The conflict in your story can be between this character and the supernatural force. One way to make a ghost story interesting is to create a scary setting for your story. In a story, **setting** refers to time and place. Popular settings for ghost stories include dark windy graveyards and old abandoned castles.

Use the chart below to help you begin. Write your ideas in point form first.

CHARACTER	SETTING	PROBLEM TO BE SOLVED
• you • you and a group of friends	• an old darkened farmhouse • an isolated lighthouse • a dark castle deep in the woods on a stormy night	• You are trapped in a building that has come alive. • A witch has tricked you into spending the night in her castle. • Your friend has been captured by some supernatural creature, and you must free him or her.

Now use your listed points to write your first draft.

Edit Your Work

A. Revise your story, using the content checklist on page 136.

B. Share your story with a partner. Try to improve your stories using these questions.
- Can I add more details describing the setting to make my story more interesting? What details might I add to increase suspense?
- Does interesting conflict occur between the main character and the supernatural creature? Can I add anything to make their struggle more intense or more interesting?

Use The Language Arts

A. Take turns reading or telling ghost stories to the rest of the class. Be sure to prepare your story carefully so you can read or tell it in a way that makes the story scary and suspenseful. You may want to darken the classroom or go to a dark room in the school. Your teacher might light one or two candles and play some spooky background music.

B. Have a class discussion: "Is it all right to tell or show scary stories to young children?"

FANTASY STORIES

Do you enjoy stories that take place in wild, fantastical worlds unlike our planet earth? Fantasy stories are based on the author's imagination. Unreal and incredible characters are created. In this excerpt, the author introduces the fantastical creature called the Iron Man.

from The iron man
by Ted Hughes

The Iron Man came to the top of the cliff.

How far had he walked? Nobody knows. Where had he come from? Nobody knows. How was he made? Nobody knows.

Taller than a house, the Iron Man stood at the top of the cliff, on the very brink, in the darkness.

The wind sang through his iron fingers. His great iron head, shaped like a dustbin but as big as a bedroom, slowly turned to the right, slowly turned to the left. His iron ears turned, this way, that way. He was hearing the sea. His eyes, like headlamps, glowed white, then red, then infra-red, searching the sea. Never before had the Iron Man seen the sea.

He swayed in the strong wind that pressed against his back. He swayed forward, on the brink of the high cliff.

And his right foot, his enormous iron right foot, lifted — up, out, into space, and the Iron Man stepped forward, off the cliff, into nothingness.

CRRRAAAASSSSSSH!

Down the cliff the Iron Man came toppling, head over heels.

CRASH!
CRASH!
CRASH!
From rock to rock, snag to snag, tumbling slowly. And as he crashed and crashed and crashed —

His iron legs fell off.

His iron arms broke off, and the hands broke off the arms.

His great iron ears fell off and his eyes fell out.

His great iron head fell off.

All the separate pieces tumbled, scattered, crashing, bumping, clanging, down onto the rocky beach far below.

A few rocks tumbled with him.

Then

Silence.

---

1. What did the Iron Man look like?
2. Why did he step off the cliff?
3. What pattern has the author used to make the story powerful?
4. What do you think will happen next in this adventure?
5. Why are we so interested in robots in our world today? Will the Iron Man be fantasy in the year 2000?

THE WRITING WORKSHOP

Get Ready

The people in a story are called **characters**. Usually the most important character in a story is known as the **hero** or **heroine**. Usually characters in stories are real people. But they can also be animals, robots, supernatural beings, or other creatures. What is the main character in "The Iron Man?"

Start Writing

Try writing a long fantasy story. Your story can take place in an unusual setting — an unusual place. Your story can be about one or more unreal and incredible characters. The plot in your story — the main events — can show how your incredible character causes a serious problem. It can tell how another character — your hero or heroine — solves this problem.

Use the chart below to help you plan your story.

CHARACTER	SETTING	PROBLEM TO BE SOLVED
• you as the hero or heroine • one or two friends of yours • one incredible character • a monster robot • Darth Vader • a giant lizard	• a mysterious planet • the depths of the ocean • a mysterious hidden valley • the world of 2050	• You are lost in the mysterious place, and are being chased by the incredible creature. • Your spaceship has been forced to land on a mysterious planet.

Use the steps below to help you write your first draft.

A. List the main events of your plot. These become the frame on which you can build your short story.

B. List the main characteristics you want each of your main characters to display.

Examples:
- height, size, build
- colour of eyes, hair, skin
- personality: quiet, shy, talkative, outgoing, serious, humorous, logical, irrational, strong, brave, kind, unkind, gentle, rough, considerate, inconsiderate, never gives up, . . .

C. List the important information about your setting.
- outdoor: geographic details, weather
- indoor: house, castle, rooms

Edit Your Work

Edit your stories in groups of four. Each person in the group can do one of the editing tasks below.

1) Proofread the sentences, looking for:
- complete thoughts
- appropriate lengths (no run-ons)
- variety — four kinds

2) Proofread the vocabulary, looking for:
- effective use of adjectives and adverbs
- effective choice of verbs
- use of similes, metaphors, alliteration, and so on

3) Proofread the mechanics, looking for:
- spelling
- punctuation
- grammar

4) Proofread for the story elements:
- Is the plot easy to follow and interesting?
- Are the setting and characters well described?
- Has suspense been used well?

Use The Language Arts

Turn your short story into a booklet. Make a suitable cover and add illustrations. Lend the class's completed booklets to another class to read.

NEWS REPORTS

Each evening, millions of people catch up on the day's news by watching the newscasts on TV. Newscasters must read the news reports as if they were talking directly to the people listening at home. The newscaster in the following excerpt is a boy called Alvin Fernald.

from **Alvin Fernald, TV anchorman**
by Clifford B. Hicks

"I've been asked by Don Brooks to appear as a guest newscaster on this station. First I want to thank him on behalf of the kids of Riverton.

"And now for the news . . .

"Flash! My investigators report that there is an absolutely secret entrance to the school. When a kid enters fourth grade, he's sworn to secrecy and told about the secret entrance by a fifth-grader.

"Flash Number Two, this one a social note. Anne Dale, who teaches fifth grade, has been secretly engaged since last Saturday night to Phil Cope, the well-known young chiropractor. The happy event occurred on Anne Dale's front-porch swing at 9:27 p.m. The Junior Newsroom joins in congratulating the happy couple."

Alvin hurried on. "Flash Number Three! You adults ought to investigate the scandal in the high-school cafeteria. A company by the name of M & R Service holds the contract to provide food for the cafeteria. The owner of M & R Service is the brother-in-law of Al Perry, who runs the cafeteria. Because the food has been so lousy, some of my high-school friends have secretly checked on the cartons when they were delivered to the school. Supposedly full cans of spaghetti sauce are only half-full."

"Good Lord, Fernald! Be careful of what you're saying," warned the voice.

"I can prove every word of it," said Alvin in a vehement whisper.

Alvin swung around, as Pete had instructed him to do, and faced another camera off to his left. "Now, short flashes from your news team, straight from the world of Riverton kids.

"A Fernald Flash! Cathy Kemp won the rope-skipping contest in Silvermont Park with a record 1 281 jumps without missing or stopping. This annual contest is sponsored by the kids of Riverton. Adults don't have anything to do with it, and that's the way it should be. Congratulations, Cathy!"

"Go ahead," said the voice in his ear. "Take all the time you want. You're doing terrific."

"Thanks," said Alvin out of the right side of his mouth.

"A Fernald Flash! Jack Wetzel now has 18 garter snakes in his collection. Flash! The robin that lives on the balcony of the library had three babies last spring. All three grew up and have joined their mother and father in the long flight south for the winter. Flash! Hepzibah Stavisloscowicz will break the sex barrier and make the junior-high football team this year. We predict she'll make a fine quarterback. We also predict the cheerleaders will have trouble with her name."

---

1. What do you think Alvin was trying to prove about kids? about adults?
2. How would you have felt if you had been Anne Dale listening to Alvin's newscast? What if you had been Al Perry?
3. When and why did the news director think that Alvin was doing a terrific job?
4. Do you think newscasts give the complete truth about a topic?

THE WRITING WORKSHOP

Get Ready

Alvin Fernald was fortunate to be asked to be a guest newscaster on the Riverton television station. He used this chance to comment on activities and problems that he saw in the community.

Start Writing

You will now have a chance to write a newscast about an activity in your community.

A. Select with your group something interesting that is happening in your community
Examples:
  • craft show
  • building that is being constructed
  • road repairs
  • sports event

B. Each person in the group can be a reporter and gather information about the event:
Examples:
  • Someone can interview people behind the scenes — planners, organizers, and so on.
  • Someone can interview people participating in the event itself — workers, artists, athletes, and so on.
  • Someone can do research about the event. He or she can try to find out:
    — How it got started
    — Why it is being carried out

C. Write down the information that your group has gathered. Decide on the order of the material. Put your material together. Create an introduction and narration that will give an overall structure to the material.

D. Create a documentary. Choose an anchorperson, on-the-scene reporters, and camera people. If you have television equipment, you can make an actual TV documentary. If not,

120

you can tape record a "radio show," or improvise a news-cast in drama.

E. If possible, include real interviews with people in the community. If not, students may play the roles of these people as if they were being interviewed.

Edit Your Work

Groups can take turns presenting their documentaries. Then the class can discuss improvements that the groups could try next time.
Examples:
- Did the audience want to know more about a person who was interviewed?
- Would more research have helped?
- Could snapshots or pictures have been used?

Use The Language Arts

A. Conduct a survey. What are the most listened to news-casts in your community?

B. 1) Think of something that happened in your community.
Examples:
- a ball game
- a parade
- an accident

2) Make up some questions about what happened.
Examples:
- Where did it take place?
- Who was there?
- What did people say?
- What did people look like?

3) Ask several people the same questions about the incident. Record their answers.

4) Compare the answers. Did everyone see and hear the same things?

COMIC STRIPS

Do you turn to the comic strips first when you read the newspaper? In only three or four frames, the comic strip artist must tell a story. If the reader knows the characters well, the artist can move the story along quickly. Do you recognize the cast of characters in these short comic strips?

For better or for worse
by Lynn Johnston

1. Can you give a reason why each of these comic strips is funny?
2. What picture of family life is presented by this artist?
3. Do comic strips exaggerate the situation, or are they realistic?
4. Conduct a survey of the class's favourite comic strips.
5. Examine a comic strip's growth over several years. For example, there have been many changes in "Peanuts" over the last ten to twenty years.

THE WRITING WORKSHOP

Get Ready

Comic strips are like cartoon films: they tell a story using words and pictures, and they do it in very little space. Lynn Johnston's comic strips remind us of our lives, since she finds funny moments like those that seem to occur in every family.

Start Writing

What would you do if you suddenly found yourself surrounded by beings from outer space? What might happen?

This situation can be the basis of a series of comic strips that you create yourself.

A. Begin by designing your aliens. (Remember, you will have to draw them.)
  - What will they look like?
  - How will they breathe? talk? move?
  - What was their habitat on their own planet?
  - Will they speak English on earth? If not, what other language or means of communication will they use?

B. Decide who else will be pictured in your comic strips?
  - Will there be human beings in the comic strips?
  - Will you be one of the characters?
  - Will the alien creatures do all the talking?

C. Choose a situation around which to build the dialogue.
  - Will the aliens be wondering about something they see on earth?
  - Will there be an argument?

D. Now you are ready to create your comic strips.
  - Draw four frames and decide on your dialogue to fill the balloons.
  - Then draw your characters.

E. Design three other strips using the same characters. Then you will have created a series of comic strips.

Edit Your Work

A. Share your comic strips with a group of other students. Check to make sure the other students understand what you meant. Will you have to change or add any words? Are your characters clearly drawn?

B. Create a scene with a partner, using one or more of your comic strips as a script. How will you portray your alien in the scene with your partner? Will you use a puppet or a mask? Will you simply roleplay the alien?

C. When you write dialogue in a story, you generally use narration as well. Make a list with your classmates of action words, or **verbs**, that can be used to introduce quotations:

    1) Kim said, "Here's the spaceship."
    2) Kim whispered, "Here's the spaceship."
    3) Kim xxxxx, "Here's the spaceship."

Use The Language Arts

A. Hold an imaginary interplanetary session to discuss how peace could be kept in the universe. Each group could invent its own alien world, and present its concerns for the future.

Groups could hold interplanetary cultural exchanges. What will your group hope to show other planets? One group from each planet could change places for a month with a group from another planet.

- What would they see?
- What mistakes would they make?
- What would they learn to do?
- What problems would they have?

Share your experiences at an interplanetary round table.

B. Make a list of descriptions of various creatures you and your classmates have read about in science fiction books.

MONOLOGUES

Do you enjoy listening to people who tell stories well? If the storyteller is speaking alone, he or she is giving a monologue. Sometimes the storyteller may pretend to be speaking to someone who is listening. In this monologue, you may recognize a familiar situation.

The missing wagon wheel
by D. Melanie Zola

I've got a wagon wheel.
I bought it last night at Steve's Milk Store.
It's for my recess.
See? It's in my lunch box —
It's gone!
My wagon wheel's gone!
Someone has stolen it.

Mrs. Butterberry! Mrs. Butterberry!
My wagon wheel is gone.
It was in my lunch box.
My lunch box was high up on the shelf.
And now my delicious wagon wheel is gone.
May everybody look for it?
Please? Please?
What cruel person would take my wagon wheel?
What a crumb!
Taking my wagon wheel out from under my very nose.
I was keeping it safe.

Did I look in my desk?
Well —
What do you know?
Here is my wagon wheel.
It was in my desk after all.
I forgot.
Sorry, Mrs. Butterberry.
Sorry, everybody.
Does anyone want a bite?
I love this wagon wheel.
I bought it last night at Steve's Milk Store.

1. What is the plot of this monologue?
2. Who do you think is speaking? Who is supposed to be listening?
3. How does the storyteller make the audience feel that other people are listening to the monologue?
4. Have you ever found yourself in a situation like this?
5. Do you remember any monologues that you have heard on records or on TV?

THE WRITING WORKSHOP

Get Ready

The speaker in "The Missing Wagon Wheel" thought someone had stolen her recess treat. But she had just misplaced it.
Has something like this ever happened to you?

Start Writing

In a monologue, only one voice speaks.

In the monologue you have just read, the author pretends
that the speaker is talking to his or her classmates and the
teacher, Mrs. Butterberry. You can write a monologue
something like this one. First you will need to decide:

1) For what situation will you create your monologue?
Examples:
- You are giving excuses for always being late.
- You are explaining why you can't go camping in the
woods.
- You are looking after a group of kindergarten children.
- You are describing an adventure on Hallowe'en.

2) What character will be giving (speaking) the
monologue?
Examples:
- yourself
- a robot
- an adult
- a very young child
- an object, not a human being

3) Who will the imaginary audience be?
Examples:
- parents
- other characters like yourself
- a policeman
- strangers
- classmates

Now you are ready to write your monologue. Begin by talking as the character. Imagine that the audience is listening. Simply write down everything you would say.

Edit Your Work

A. Now that you have the monologue done in rough, you can begin to shape it.

1) Does it have an opening that will attract people's attention?

2) Does it have an ending that will summarize your monologue? The ending might also make people laugh or surprise them.

3) Have you made clear who your imaginary audience is?

B. Monologues are written in the **first person**: that is, they use *I* or *we*. The writer pretends to be the main character in the monologue. Suppose you wanted to change a monologue to make it a story about somebody else. You could do so by using the **third person**. That is, you would use *he*, *she*, or *they*.

Try rewriting part of "The Missing Wagon Wheel" or your own monologue in the third person. Use *he, she,* or *they* in place of *I* or *we*. How does this change the monologue?

Use The Language Arts

Prepare and give an oral presentation of your monologue to a group or to the whole class.

SCRIPTS

When you watch a movie, it is easy to forget that the film must begin with a written script. The script writer creates the story, the action, and the characters. He or she writes dialogue and directions for the actors and camera people to follow. As you read the following movie script, notice how it is different from a stage script.

from Raiders of the lost ark
A Lucasfilm

FADE IN:
(Title and credits fade in and out during the following sequence.)

EXTERIOR: SOUTH AMERICA — HIGH JUNGLE — DAY

Mountain peak against sky in dense, lush rain forests filled with the varied sounds of the jungle. Ragged, jutting canyon walls are half-hidden by the thick mists. A group of men make their way along a narrow trail across the green face of the canyon.

At the head of the party is an American, INDIANA JONES. Behind him come some QUECHUA INDIANS. Bringing up the rear are two Spanish Peruvians, SATIPO and BARRANCA.

An Indian chops at a branch and is faced with a horrific stone sculpture. The Indian screams and runs away as birds fly out from the undergrowth. Indy steps forward quickly and gazes at the sculpture as more birds fly out. Satipo and Barranca exchange looks, then glance over their shoulders as they move on.

Indy leads Satipo and Barranca along a stream towards heavy mist. Visibility is cut to about two metres.

As Indy jumps the stream, he sees a short dart sticking from

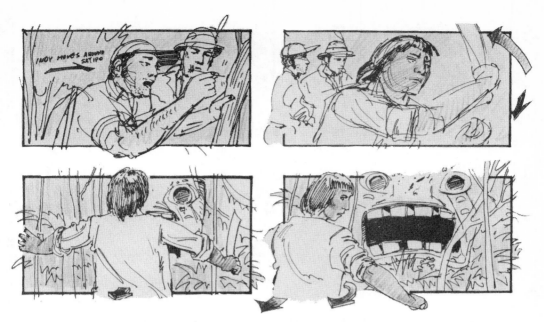

a tree. He extracts it, fingering its point, then drops it and moves on. Barranca and Satipo run forward and Satipo picks up the dart. He tastes his fingers and spits.

(Credits end.)

Satipo: The Hovitos are near. The poison is still fresh . . . three days. They're following us.

Barranca: If they knew we were here, they would have killed us already.

Indy walks through shafts of light in thick forest and Satipo and Barranca follow. SUBTITLE fades in:

SOUTH AMERICA
1936

Standing in front of a waterfall, Indy pulls out a torn, aged piece of parchment, then takes a second piece from Satipo and fits them together . . .

 Indy steps forward from the shadows and we see his face for the first time. He walks up a hill to the face of the vegetation-enshrouded TEMPLE OF THE CHACHAPOYAN WARRIORS, 2 000 years old. He quickly ducks inside, then reappears as Satipo catches up, carrying a backpack.

 Indy pulls a bag from the pack and bends down, starting to fill it with sand.

Indy: This is it. This is where Forrestal cashed in.
Satipo: A friend of yours?
Indy: A competitor. He was good. He was very, very good.

Indy tucks the bag of sand into the waist of his pants.

Satipo: Señor, nobody's come out of there alive! Please?

Indy turns Satipo around, pulls a small shovel from the pack, and throws the pack to the ground.

INTERIOR: TEMPLE — INCLINED PASSAGE — DAY

Indy and Satipo, who carries a torch, walk up the slightly inclined, tubular passage from the main entrance. Indy wipes away thick spiderwebs with his whip.
   As he steps out of a shadow, three huge black tarantulas are crawling up the back of his jacket. He doesn't notice them and disappears into another shadow. When he emerges, Satipo sees the tarantulas and stops, terrified.

Satipo *(hoarsely):* Señor!

Indy looks at him, sees what he's pointing at, and casually brushes off all three spiders with his rolled whip, as he would a fly. Satipo sees one on his own shoulders and, unable to speak, works his jaw silently. Satipo pirouettes slowly — his back is covered with tarantulas. They crawl over his chest, neck, and back. Indy flicks them to the ground and they scuttle away.

---

1. Why is there so little dialogue in this script?
2. How is a film script different from a stage script?
3. Why do people enjoy adventure films and books?
4. What film scripts would you like to read?
5. In groups, act out the narration that describes what the people are doing in the film.

THE WRITING WORKSHOP

Get Ready

In this excerpt from the film script of *Raiders of the Lost Ark*, you have read both the dialogue that the actors speak and the narration that describes what is happening on the screen. These two items make up what is called a *film scenario*.

Start Writing

In writing a scenario, you have to paint **word pictures** of what the audience would be seeing. As well, you have to create the **dialogue** for the actors to speak.

A. Brainstorm, as a class, ideas for an adventure film.
- Where will it take place?
- Who will be the hero or heroes?
- Who will be the villain or villains?
- What terrible things will happen during the adventure?
- What quest is the hero on? (Sometimes it is fun not to decide on the ending at this point.)

B. Divide the scenario-writing among members of the class. You could work alone or with a group. Assign each part of the scenario that the class has brainstormed.

C. Complete the writing of the separate incidents. Each part should be about a page long. It should be composed of descriptive narration and dialogue. You may want to indicate some of the camera shots to build suspense.

Examples:
- close up
- medium shot
- long shot

D. You could have two different endings written. The class could choose which they like better, once the scenario is put together.

Edit Your Work

A. Each section of the scenario can be shared with the class. Everyone will have to make slight changes so that the whole scenario will go together, and there will be a feeling of one single film.
- Is there enough dialogue so that the audience will understand the story of the film?
- Are settings explained in enough detail?
- Does the story build to a climax?
- Should any of the scenes be rearranged?

B. Make any changes that the class feels are needed.

C. Choose and add the ending. Adjust it as needed.

Use The Language Arts

A. Find a copy of a film script in a library or bookstore. Choose one section of the script and practise it as a small play. Share your scene with the class and see if they can tell which movie you are rehearsing.

B. Make a film by using only your imagination. Concentrate on recreating the thoughts of someone who is in the middle of an exciting situation. Pretend to be the person. Talk to yourself about what is happening to you at this time. Write down (or tape record) everything you think. Write quickly, and use the first words that come to your mind. Tell how things look, and how they sound.
Examples:
- Record your thoughts as a hockey goalie between periods.
- Record your thoughts as an astronaut before landing on a strange planet.
- Record your thoughts as a fashion model during your first fashion show.

Revise your final "spontaneous film" script and let your classmates read it.

Content Checklist

1) Did I say what I wanted to say?

2) Did I say it clearly so that others would understand what I wrote?

3) Did I include all the necessary information?

4) Did I write all the events or steps in order?

5) If I was asked to follow a pattern, did I do it well?

6) Did I use the most interesting and most accurate words I could think of?

7) Did I write a good beginning, middle, and end?

8) If writing a paragraph, did I write a strong topic sentence? Do all of the other sentences in the paragraph belong with the topic sentence?

9) Did I use comparisons to make my work more interesting and more accurate?

Proofreading Checklist

1) Does each sentence make sense?

2) Have I used capital letters correctly?

3) Have I punctuated each sentence properly?

4) Did I spell words correctly, checking those I was unsure about?

5) Did I use proper form with regard to indenting, titles, and margins?

6) Is my handwriting clear and easy to read?

Editorial Group Checklist

Edit your work in a group. Each group member can take one editing job. Decide which member will:

1) Check to see that each sentence makes sense.

2) Check to see that capital letters and punctuation marks have been used correctly.

3) Check to see that each word is spelled correctly.

4) Check to see that proper form was used with regard to indenting, titles, and margins.

AUTHOR/TITLE INDEX

SUBJECT INDEX

ACKNOWLEDGMENTS

Every effort has been made to acknowledge all sources of material used in this book. The publishers would be grateful if any errors or omissions were pointed out, so that they may be corrected.

Acknowledgment is gratefully made for the use of the following copyright material: "About Nothing" by Jack Boulogne, by permission of the author. "The Base Stealer" copyright © 1948 by Robert Francis. Reprinted from *The Orb Weaver* by permission of Wesleyan University Press. This poem first appeared in *Forum*. Excerpts from *The Biggest Tongue Twister Book in the World* by Gyles Brandreth © Gyles Brandreth 1978. By permission of the author. Excerpt from *A Child in Prison Camp* by permission of Tundra Books, Montreal. Excerpts from *Children's Choices of Canadian Books, Volume 1 (1979), Volume 2 (1981)*, and *Volume 3 (1983)*, edited by Margaret Caughey; used by permission of the Citizens' Committee on Children, P.O. Box 6133, Station J, Ottawa, K2A 1T2. "Comin' Down the Chimney," traditional, with adapted lyrics by Raffi. Arranged by Raffi and Ken Whiteley. Copyright © 1980 Homeland Publishing (CAPAC). All rights reserved. Used by permission. "Cup Berth up for Grabs" copyright © *The Canadian Press*, 1983. Used by permission. Excerpt from *The Dictionary of Imaginary Places* by Alberto Manguel and Gianni Guadalupi (1980). Reprinted by permission of the authors. "Dragons" from *The Book of Weird*, reprinted by permission of Curtis Brown Associates, Ltd. Copyright © 1967 by Barbara Ninde Byfield. "Eels Helped over Dam" copyright © *The Canadian Press*. Used by permission. Excerpt from *Everybody Needs a Rock* by Byrd Baylor. Copyright © 1974 by Byrd Baylor. Reprinted with permission of Charles Scribner's Sons. "Fauna Canadiana" by Meguido Zola, by permission of the author. "For Better or for Worse" cartoons copyright 1980, 1982, 1983, Universal Press Syndicate. Reprinted with permission. All rights reserved. Excerpt from *From A to Z: The Collected Letters of Irene and Hallie Coletta* by Irene Coletta. Published by Prentice-Hall, Inc., copyright © 1979. Reprinted by permission of the author and illustrator. "Grocery List" © 1974 by William Cole. Used by permission. "The Hippopotamus at Dinner" and the accompanying illustration from *Fables*, written and illustrated by Arnold Lobel. Copyright © 1980 by Arnold Lobel. Used by permission of Harper & Row, Publishers, Inc. "How Trouble Made the Monkey Eat Pepper" published with permission of Kids Can Press, Toronto, Canada. Text © Rita Cox. Excerpt from *The Iron Man* by Ted Hughes reprinted by permission of Faber and Faber Ltd. "Jellyfish" by Patrick Lashmar, by permission of the author. Excerpt from *Julie of the Wolves* by Jean Craighead George copyright © 1972 by Jean Craighead George. Used by permission of Harper & Row, Publishers, Inc. "The Missing Wagon Wheel" © D. Melanie Zola, by permission of the author. Excerpt from *Once There Were Dragons* by John Mole used by permission of Andre Deutsch, copyright © 1979. Excerpt from *Pioneer Girl*. Reprinted by permission of McGraw-Hill Ryerson Limited. Excerpt from *A Prairie Boy's Summer* by William Kurelek by permission of Tundra Books, Montreal. Excerpt from *The Pushcart War* by Jean Merrill, © 1964 by Jean Merrill. A Young Scott Book. Published by Addison-Wesley, Reading, Massachusetts. Reprinted with permission of the publisher. Excerpt from *Raiders of the Lost Ark* © Lucasfilm Ltd. (LFL) 1981. All rights reserved. Used by courtesy of Lucasfilm Ltd. Excerpt from *Robbers, Bones and Mean Dogs* by Barry & Velma Berkey. Text copyright © 1978 by Barry & Velma Berkey. Illustration © 1978 by Marilyn Hofner. Published by Addison-Wesley, Reading, Massachusetts. Reprinted with permission of the publisher. "The Special Gift" from *George and Martha: Tons of Fun* by James Marshall. Copyright © 1980 by James Marshall. Reprinted by permission of Houghton Mifflin Company. "What Is This?" © Miriam Young. Used by permission of Peter Young. Excerpt from *Wild Mouse* by Irene Brady. Copyright © 1976, 1974 Irene Brady. Reprinted with the permission of Charles Scribner's Sons.